Orrest
Head

WINDERMERE

WINDERMERE

AMBLESIDE.

RYDAL WATER

GRASMERE

GRASMERE.

Pavey Ark

Langdale
Bowfell Pikes
Buttress
Bowfell Gimmer Crag
Bowfell

Wrynose Pass

CONISTON

CONISTON

CONISTON

Coniston
Old Man
Crag
Dow Crag
Goats
Water

Hardknott Pass

Lingmell
Scafell Pikes
Mickledore
Scafell

Yewb

WASTWATER

The Screes

THE
LAKE DISTRICT

1 Km
5 miles

Camera on the Crags

Camera on the Crags

a portfolio of early rock climbing photographs by the Abraham Brothers

Selected and written by
Alan Hankinson

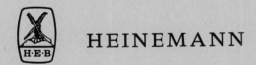
HEINEMANN

Heinemann Educational Books Ltd
LONDON EDINBURGH MELBOURNE AUCKLAND TORONTO
HONG KONG SINGAPORE KUALA LUMPUR
IBADAN NAIROBI JOHANNESBURG
LUSAKA NEW DELHI

ISBN O 435 86000 3
© Alan Hankinson 1975
First published 1975

Published by Heinemann Educational Books Ltd
48 Charles Street, London W1X 8AH
Filmset and printed in Great Britain by BAS Printers Limited, Wallop, Hampshire
and bound by Hunter & Foulis Ltd, Edinburgh

Acknowledgments

Most of the photographs in this book are taken from negatives which belong to the Fell and Rock Climbing Club of the English Lake District. A few—mostly those taken in the Western Highlands of Scotland—are in the possession of Mr George Fisher of Keswick. I am greatly indebted to both for making the negatives available to me, and especially to Mr F. H. F. Simpson of the Fell and Rock Climbing Club for his unfailing help. The cinéfilm stills are from Pathé Review and I am grateful to E.M.I. Film Distributors Ltd. for permission to reproduce them.

Prints were made from the original negatives by Mrs Jackie O'Lochlainn.

The section about the Abrahams' camera owes much to Mr Arthur Dawson who demonstrated the camera and Chris Bonington who took the photographs.

A number of people gave generous help with the research—Mr H. R. C. Carr, Mr T. S. Blakeney, Mr Edward C. Pyatt and the late Sir Claude Elliott. Mr. Tony Moulam helped me to identify some of the more baffling locations; Mr Chris Briggs gave me access to the 'Locked Book' at the Pen-y-Gwryd hotel; and Mr Frank Singleton, librarian of *The Guardian* in Manchester, hunted down some relevant cuttings. I would also thank Methuen & Co. Ltd. for permission to quote from George Abraham's book, *Mountain Adventures at Home and Abroad*.

The labour of research was lightened—transformed, indeed, into a pleasure—by the help I was given by two branches of the Abraham family in Keswick. Mrs Enid Wilson, George Abraham's daughter, went to great trouble to acquaint me with the family history. And Ashley's son, Mr Geoffrey P. Abraham, and his wife Mary were at all times hospitable and encouraging and informative. I deeply regret that Mr Abraham, to whom this book is affectionately dedicated, died before its completion.

I was encouraged throughout—from the birth of the idea of this book at his house in Borrowdale—by the keen interest and enthusiasm of my publisher, Mr Alan Hill.

My greatest debt, as always, is to my wife who kept the coffee flowing and did the typing and much of the administrative work and compiled the index and, most important of all, kept a critical eye on style and content at every stage.

Contents

		page
ACKNOWLEDGEMENTS		iv
1.	Forming the Partnership	1
2.	The Abraham Background	6
3.	The Birth of Rock Climbing	8
4.	The Partnership in Action	11
5.	Publication and Controversy	16
6.	The Evangelical Years	20
7.	Photographic Methods	24
8.	The Later Years	27
PLATES		*following* page
The People		29
The Lake District		29
Snowdonia		33
Scotland		37
An Excursion into Filming		39
How the Camera Works		39
INDEX		41

To
Geoff Abraham

1 Forming the Partnership

In one of his books George Abraham, the elder of the climber-photographer brothers, described an encounter that was to play a formative role in their careers:

> My first meeting with Owen Glynne Jones was during the Easter holidays of 1896. Without any foreword he called on us in Keswick in the early hours of a beautiful April morning after a long journey from town. In two hours' time mutual keenness had promoted friendship, parental misgivings had been overcome, and we were off to Wastdale.

George was twenty-five and his brother Ashley was six years younger when O. G. Jones landed with such characteristic éclat in their lives. They were the sons of Mr George Perry Abraham, a respected citizen of Keswick in the Lake District where he ran a successful photography business. The brothers were vigorous and adventurous and had already done a good deal of hard scrambling and some rock climbing chiefly on the crags around Keswick, and Ashley had met Jones at least once before, the previous Christmas, when he was one of a large group which attempted a gully climb on Scafell in deep snow. Both brothers would have heard stories of Jones' climbing prowess—his gymnastic suppleness, the remarkable strength of his arms and fingers, and the high daring of routes he had been making on the cliffs around Wasdale Head. They must have been flattered and thrilled to have been picked out by this already almost legendary man as his companions for a day's climbing.

It turned out to be an eventful day, as days in the hills with O. G. Jones frequently did. The three young men—Jones was twenty-eight—walked up Borrowdale and on to Sty Head Pass where they met John Wilson Robinson, one of the leading pioneers of rock climbing in the previous decade. According to George's account, it was a moment of some drama:

> The sight of Kern Knotts turned the conversation in that direction. Robinson held strong views about the unwisdom of making the ascent of Kern Knotts Crack. It was then unclimbed, and he urged that its conquest would lead to unjustifiable attempts by other less skilful climbers, and disaster would result. Jones disagreed. I remember Robinson's last 'Parthian shot' as he turned towards Borrowdale. 'Well, Jones,' he said, smiling, 'if you climb that crack, I'll never speak to you again.'

Jones had in fact already reconnoitred part of the Crack (Plate 44) but he refrained from mentioning this to Robinson, and he did not, on this occasion, attempt the climb. He wanted to test the metal of his new companions and it must have been clear, even to him, that he could hardly begin by attempting an unclimbed route of such patent severity. The test he had in mind was exacting enough. With the two brothers he walked along the path past Kern Knotts to the foot of the Napes ridges of Great Gable and then, in under two hours, led them up the three great ridge climbs there, Eagle's Nest, Needle Ridge and the Arrowhead. This was powerful going by any standard. Eagle's Nest Ridge (Plates 42 and 43) was the hardest route then made and is still graded 'Very Severe (Mild)' in the climbers' guide book.

Jones was more than satisfied with the brothers' performance, and they were deeply impressed. George later wrote:

> That first day with Owen Glynne Jones meant much more than wrestling with those glorious crags, every muscle and sense alive to instant action as to method of rope and rock-work. Our real selves stood revealed, and a friendship was formed which proved in after years to be the most valuable possession of life.

What they formed that April day in 1896 was not only a friendship and a climbing partnership. It became a business partnership too. Almost certainly there was some element of calculation in Jones' arrival on the Abraham doorstep that Easter morning. He had been climbing seriously for six years, continuously developing his skill in the Lake District and North Wales and in the Alps. He had kept a detailed short-hand diary of his adventures. Two years earlier he had introduced Walter Parry Haskett Smith, the man who more than any other could claim to have invented rock climbing, to some of the Welsh routes and helped him in the preparation and writing of the second volume of his climbing guides. Now Jones was planning his own book and it would be very different.

The Haskett Smith volumes are little more than lists of the scrambling and climbing grounds to be found in England, Wales and Ireland, arranged alphabetically and packed with information about locations and climbing history, etymology and local lore. They are factual, accurate, and, for the period, comprehensive. But they are also dry and academic. It is only rarely that Haskett Smith allows his personality to peep through and give some evocative detail about a climb or some hint of what it must have felt like to be exploring the crags in those heady days when a whole fresh field of adventure was being opened up.

Owen Glynne Jones was the man to redress the balance. Although an academic by profession—he taught physics at the City of London School—he was by nature, perhaps because of his Celtic origins, a man of temperament and imagination, a powerful and ebullient personality. To him climbing was adventure or it was nothing. It was a double exploration, of new ways up the cliffs and of the limits of his own capabilities, physical and mental. 'A line must be drawn somewhere,' he wrote, 'to separate the possible from the impossible, and some try to draw it by their own experience.'

Jones was foremost in the 1890s among those who made the attempt and the first to seek to express in writing all the anxieties and exhilarations, the dangers and difficulties and set-backs as well as the joys of comradeship and conquest, which attended the attempt. His own fast-flowing narrative style would undoubtedly do much to make his book an exciting and vivid reflection of his feelings. But its effect would clearly be considerably strengthened by photographs of the crags and the rock routes and of climbers in action. He knew the power of a good photograph. According to his own account he had been inspired to attempt Napes Needle five years earlier by chance sighting, in a shop window in the Strand, of Professor Dixon's photograph of climbers on that photogenic pinnacle. Such considerations undoubtedly lay at the back of his mind—and probably not so far back—when he sought out the company of the Abraham brothers, already climbers of enthusiasm and some skill and already trained to play an active part in their father's business.

Within a few days they were taking their equipment with them into the mountains, an Underwood whole-plate camera, a tripod, two lenses and a dozen glass-plate negatives, a total weight of over twenty pounds with the combined disadvantages of being both cumbersome and fragile. Jones gives a cheerful account in his book of the extra problems involved by photography. On April 20th they decided to follow a route made three years earlier from Deep Ghyll to the top of Scafell Pinnacle. Jones led off up the long curving crack, with George Abraham second. When he gained the niche at the top of the crack, he paused to survey the possibilities ahead and found them discouraging:

Direct progress upwards seemed quite impossible; a feasible traverse over some badly-sloping moss-covered ledges to the right led to the sky-line at a spot where the *arête* made a vertical spring upwards for forty feet. A descent would have been seriously difficult, but it was the one thing we did not want. I could hear another climbing party finishing an ascent of the pinnacle by the ordinary route, their voices echoing down the ghyll and cheering me with a sense of neighbourliness. George and Ashley were holding an animated discussion below on the subject of photography. The light was excellent, and our positions most artistic. The cameras were left in the cave at the foot of the ghyll. Ashley was afraid I meant to go up without him; but his professional instinct got the better of his desire to climb, and, shouting out to us to stay where we were for five minutes, he ran round to the high-level traverse on the other side of the ghyll, and down the Lord's Rake to the cavern.

George had the tripod screw and could not hand it to his brother; so, asking me to hold him firmly with the rope, he practised throwing stones across the gully to the traverse. Then, tying the screw to a stone, he managed to project this over successfully. We composed our limbs to a photographic quiescence. Ashley had a splendid wide-angle lens, which from his elevated position on the traverse opposite could take in 400 feet of the cliff, showing the entire route to the summit. It was his turn to take the lead. 'Mr. Jones! I can't see you, your clothes are so dark.' I apologized. 'Will you step out a foot or two from that hole?' I was in a cheerful mood and ready to oblige a friend, but the platform was scarcely two feet square, and to acquiesce was to step out a few hundred feet into Deep Ghyll. For this I had not made adequate preparation and told him so. 'Well, will you take off your coat?' That I could do with pleasure, and for a while his instructions were levelled at George.

He was in an awkward place and was much cramped in ensuring safety, but

Ashley was dissatisfied and insisted on his lifting the left leg. This gave him no foot-hold to speak of, but in the cause of photography he had been trained to manage without such adventitious aids. He grumbled a little at the inconvenience but obeyed, resolving that if he were living when the next slide was to be exposed he himself would be the manipulator and his brother the centre of the picture. The ghyll had become rather gloomy and we had a lengthy exposure. I was glad to slip on my Norfolk again and draw in the rope for George's ascent.

Ashley's photograph can be seen on Plate 32. After taking the picture he abandoned the camera and tripod and roped up to join the others on a climb which soon became a new route when Jones, either through short-sightedness or his strong urge towards innovation, discovered a harder variant of the original. It became so difficult that they were forced to resort to the 'combined operation' tactics which were to stand them in useful stead on many subsequent ascents. At one point Jones had to climb onto Ashley's shoulder to reach acceptable holds. A little further up they gathered on an uncomfort-able ledge:

It shelved badly downwards and offered no guarantee of safety in case I fell from the next vertical bit. But George sturdily rammed his brother close against the wall and intimated that the two would accept the responsibility of fielding me if necessary. I mounted their shoulders and reached up at arms' length to a sharp and firm edge of rock. A preliminary grind of my boot into a shoulder-blade and then a clear swing out on the arms, a desperate pull-up with knees and toes vainly seeking support, and at last the upper shelf was mounted.

The climb, Jones' Route from Deep Ghyll, is today graded 'Severe (Mild)'.

Two days later they were tackling something more difficult, Collier's Climb on Scafell Crag, and though they do not seem to have taken the camera with them this time, Ashley's shoulders and head were called into service as footholds. Near the top, the worst difficulties overcome, Jones felt triumphant:

The situation was certainly a trying one, for a downward gaze could only take in the rib of rock immediately below and the distant screes 200 feet beyond. I flung some loose stones far out into space, and could only just hear a faint clatter as they touched the scree. Now was the time to appreciate the joy of climbing, in perfect health, with perfect weather, and in a difficult place without danger, and I secretly laughed as I called to the others that the outlook was terribly bad and that our enterprise must be given up. But they also laughed, and told me to go higher and change my mind, for they knew by the tone that my temper was unruffled. A few feet more and I drew up to the platform.

The weather stayed fine throughout the holiday and on sound dry rock, in the spring sunshine, the friendship was formed. They were to have only three years together, and even in that brief period they were able to climb together only occasionally. Despite this, theirs was to prove one of the great creative partnerships in the history of rock climbing, partly through the new routes they made in the Lake District and North Wales, and partly through their pioneering work in publicising the sport.

Jones' book, *Rock Climbing in the English Lake District*, was published at the end of the following year and was illustrated by thirty full-page reproductions of Abraham photographs. It was an immediate success and became a classic, the definitive portrait of the spirit of the days when rock climbing was young. Jones' personality was too strong to be subdued by the printed word. His climbing was whole-hearted and bold. 'He was never so happy,' the brothers said, 'as when in a really tight place.' He was what the rock climbing world came to call, some fifty years later, 'a hard man', prepared to tackle formidable new problems in all kinds of conditions, under ice or snow, through waterfalls, in blizzards or in gales. He regularly lost his way and his expeditions often ended with the party staggering home in the dark from some totally unintended direction. He fell off a good deal but always bounced back, more determined than ever. And the spirit of the man shines through his writing and makes his book, for all its dated style and the occasional touch of melodrama, exciting reading to this day.

The Abraham photographs, which this book celebrates, have also become classics. Eleven of the pictures which appeared in Jones' book are reproduced in this. And in the years that followed the brothers took hundreds more: mountain landscapes in the Lake District, North Wales and Scotland, and also in the Alps and the Dolomites; pictures of rock scenery, the climbers' routes on the crags; and, best of all perhaps, pictures of climbers in action. Over the next thirty or so years the brothers built up, negative by careful negative, an incomparable portrait of the youthful years of rock climbing. And they became, chiefly through the photographs but also by virtue of their books and lectures and even films, the leading evangelists of the sport in the first quarter of this century.

If the brothers had been born a little earlier and gone to Wasdale Head, say, a dozen years sooner, when Haskett Smith and J. W. Robinson were making their exploratory expeditions on the cliffs of Scafell and Pillar Rock and Great Gable, then the Abraham pictorial record would have been complete. Even so it must be counted as highly fortunate, if not entirely fortuitous, that they joined forces with O. G. Jones at the moment when they had learned their photographic skills, when he was at the peak of his powers, and when rock climbing was still new and fresh and rapidly developing.

2 The Abraham Background

The father of the Abraham brothers and founder of the Keswick photography business, George Perry Abraham, was born in Wiltshire in the 1830s. Orphaned early in life, he was brought up by his mother's parents, the Perrys, who ran a market garden in Devizes. When he was in his mid-teens they sent him to London to serve an apprenticeship with Elliott and Fry, a photographic firm in Baker Street. It was an enterprising thing to do. Photography was still a new science in the middle of the last century, although it had advanced enormously in the twenty-five years since its invention and already men like Roger Fenton and James Robertson were showing, in the Crimea, how effective it could be.

Sometime around 1860 George Perry Abraham completed his apprenticeship and went north to Keswick to try his luck as a journeyman-photographer. He worked for four years for an established photographer of the town, Alfred Pettit. Then, to his surprise, he was given notice as the summer season drew to its close. He decided to set up on his own, secured the backing of a couple of local businessmen, and began, modestly enough, in a wooden hut on the corner of Lake Road and Borrowdale Road, the site where a petrol station now stands. From here he sold 'while-you-wait' photographs called 'Tintypes' to the passing public. This happened in 1865 and he must have done remarkably well, or found additional backing, because he was able to buy a plot on the other side of Lake Road, which was all open fields at that time, and build the substantial shop which is still there, though greatly modified of late. He moved into the new premises and launched his business career proper in 1866.

He was an able photographer and soon proved a good businessman as well, and as the years went by he became a respected and devoted Keswickian. He was a regular worshipper at the Congregational church and a pillar of the choir. He was elected to Keswick Urban District Council and served on it for many years. He was a keen and active Freemason. Shortly after he had established the shop he married a Penrith girl, Mary Dixon, the daughter of a senior engineer of the Cockermouth, Keswick and Penrith Railway company. They had five children. George, the eldest, was born in 1870; next a daughter, Ida; then, in 1876, Ashley arrived; and after him came two more sons, Sidney and John. The children were sent to a small private school in Keswick, Blackman's School, and George later went to Manchester to the Grammar School and then to study art.

The two oldest boys were destined from the start to go into the family business and neither seems to have resented it at the time or ever subsequently regretted it. They loved the Lake District—George regarded his time in Manchester as an exile—and they were soon exploring the fells around their home and venturing further and further away from the tourists' paths and onto rougher and steeper ground. It was not long before they were experimenting with mountain photography too. The photograph on Plate 8 must be among the first they ever took, and is certainly the earliest that has survived in negative form. It was taken in 1890 and the evidence suggests that the photographer was Ashley, who must have been about fourteen at the time. At this early stage, the brothers' photographic techniques were immeasurably ahead of their climbing techniques.

For a few years in the early 1890s George and Ashley explored alone on the then-unfashionable cliffs around Keswick. They climbed Sandbed Ghyll in St. John's in the Vale. In 1892 they made the first recorded rock climb in Borrowdale, Walla Crag Gully, which the current guide book grades 'Difficult' and describes as 'an unpleasant route with much vegetation.' They conquered Dollywaggon Gully in Grisedale. But there is no record of either of them coming into contact with the mainstream of the sport, which was already flowing strongly only a dozen miles away at Wasdale Head, until the Christmas of 1895, when Ashley found himself a member of a large party following Owen Glynne Jones up to Deep Ghyll on Scafell. Jones wrote of the occasion:

We had a great deal of very soft snow to get through on our way up, and I was looking forward to a long halt in the lower cave, where we should at least be protected from the wind and snow. Great was our distress when we found the entrance completely blocked up by a huge drift. It must have been fully twenty feet deep in front of the cave, and the prospect was most disheartening. In disgust I clambered up the wall immediately to the right of the boulder, and at last managed to reach the aperture leading into the cave from above. It was festooned with huge icicles, and at first the entrance looked effectually blocked. Smashing down the ice with the energy of despair, the tremendous clatter suggesting to my friends that of a bull in a hardware shop, I discovered that the chimney was only iced at its entrance, and that the upper storey of the cave could be reached. Some of the others quickly followed, and we found ourselves in a spacious chamber into which the great heap of snow had scarcely encroached. This was delightful. We threw ourselves into the drift that blocked the main entrance, and cut away at it with vigour till at last we had tunnelled through to the daylight. The biggest man of the party yet remained outside and we persuaded him to insert his legs into the aperture. Without giving him time to change his mind we seized his boots and hauled hard. For one dread moment we thought him jammed for ever, but immediately afterwards we found ourselves lying on our backs in the cave with a yawning opening in the snowdrift, the while our massive friend measured his diminished circumference with a loop of rope.

The 'massive friend' was Ashley. Not yet twenty, he was already a man of considerable girth.

Four months after this Jones collected the brothers from Keswick and swept them into the rock climbing world.

3 The Birth of Rock Climbing

There were three good reasons why Wasdale Head became the focal point for the first rock climbers. It gave easy access to the most challenging cliffs of the Lake District: Great Gable immediately above the valley head; Scafell Crag to the south; and three miles or so to the north, Pillar Rock. Secondly, it was then, as it remains to this day, one of the least accessible dale heads of the District and so was spared the incursion of the tourist droves. And finally, in the Wastwater Hotel, it could offer a hostelry big enough to accommodate most of the climbing community at any given moment in some comfort and presided over by a cheerful, capable and ever-tolerant landlord, Dan Tyson. The same happy coincidence of location and landlord had made the Pen-y-Gwryd Hotel in Snowdonia, under the presidency of Harry Owen, the natural gathering-place for the North Wales pioneers.

As a continuing and developing passion, rock climbing emerged in the 1880s. Men had, of course, clambered up difficult rock routes long before that time but only in an isolated and haphazard way. The forbidding cliff of Clogwyn du'r Arddu (Plate 74) on the flank of Snowdon was climbed, along the narrow ledge of the East Terrace, by two plant-hunting botanists in 1798. Four years later the poet-philosopher, Samuel Taylor Coleridge, took a short cut from the summit of Scafell to Mickledore by way of what is now called Broad Stand. In 1826 a Lakeland shepherd, John Atkinson, became the first person to reach the top of Pillar Rock, and, in the decades that followed, the ascent of Pillar, by the Old West Route or the Slab and Notch on its eastern face, became a popular excursion for the adventurously inclined. Then, after the mid-century discovery of the delights of Alpine mountaineering by a few upper-class English gentlemen, some of them took to using the snow-filled gullies of the British cliffs as a winter practice ground for their step cutting.

But it was not until the arrival of Walter Parry Haskett Smith at Wasdale Head that rock climbing, as a separate entity, really got under way. He went there in 1881 with an undergraduate reading party from Oxford, was introduced to rough scrambling by the veteran hill-wanderer, F. H. Bowring, and returned the next year with his younger brother to attack and conquer some of the easier gully routes on Great End, Pavey Ark, Bowfell Buttress, Gimmer Crag and Pillar Rock. The habit was established and in the next few years Haskett Smith led the way onto increasingly difficult climbs and gathered around him a growing band of enthusiasts.

They had many difficulties to overcome. The accumulated debris of the ages lay along their routes. They had to test every hold for its staying power and clear away loose boulders and stones and all the slimy and uncertain vegetation that had taken root in the cracks and crevices. Most of their contemporaries regarded them as crazy and many Alpine Club men, those who considered mountaineering exclusively a matter of snow and ice routes on big mountains, dismissed them contemptuously as 'chimney-sweeps' and 'rock gymnasts'. Furthermore, their equipment and techniques were primitive. They wore thick tweeds and country boots, heavily studded with nails. In 1885 two local men, John Wilson Robinson of Lorton and George Seatree of Penrith, introduced the Alpine rope to Cumberland climbing and, though it was soon in general use, it was many years before safety techniques of any reliability were evolved. They often climbed simultaneously which meant that if one man fell off, all those roped to him would be pulled off with him. In addition to all this, and perhaps most telling of all, they were venturing into a completely new realm of human experience, putting themselves to a test that man had never attempted before, pushing back the line which separates the possible from the impossible.

Yet the record of their achievements is impressive. At first they concentrated on the gullies, the wide clefts which offered the lines of least resistance up the cliffs, where the stretches of actual climbing tended to be short, the ledges commodious and where the dark containing walls gave a reassurance of security, however misleading. But they soon became more ambitious. In June 1886 Haskett Smith, on his own, scaled Napes Needle (Plate 36), the short but shapely pinnacle on the south side of Great Gable. Next year three of the five brilliant Hopkinson brothers from Manchester descended the face of Scafell Pinnacle and set up their cairn on a ledge 250 feet above the screes. And the year after that a redoubtable Yorkshireman, Cecil Slingsby, the pioneer of Norwegian mountaineering, led the chimney route on the Pinnacle which still bears his name. Formidable new recruits were now joining in. In April 1892 Godfrey Solly, a quiet solicitor from Birkenhead, led Eagle's Nest Ridge on Great Gable. The following Christmas a distinguished man of science, Professor Norman Collie, solved the long-standing problem of Moss Ghyll on Scafell (Plate 33). And soon after that a Manchester surgeon, Dr Joseph Collier, forced a route on Scafell, Collier's Climb, which is still graded 'Severe (Hard)'.

These are only the highlights of that productive period. Many other routes were made and many subtle variations of established routes. And this was achieved without a single fatal accident over a period of more than 20 years and in a holiday spirit.

The rock climbing community which flourished at Wasdale Head in the late 1880s and throughout the 1890s was small, predominantly masculine, intensely dedicated to the development of the sport, highly companionable, and happy. For a few days each Christmas, Easter and Whitsun, they took over the Wastwater Hotel (Plates 12 and 13). During the hours of daylight they were on the crags, forcing new routes or introducing their friends to old favourites. Each evening, their boots and ropes abandoned in the hall and their wet stockings and tweeds steaming in the drying room, they would discuss their day's exploits or reminisce about former adventures or dispute the finer points of technique while the more energetic spirits adjourned to the billiard room to engage in violent games and contests of strength and gymnastic skill. They ate heartily, drank sparingly and enjoyed themselves hugely.

The sport attracted men of the professional middle class, many of them university educated, most of them city-dwellers—scientists, engineers, doctors, lawyers, businessmen and teachers. They were hard-working and successful men, usually family men, and they found in these short mountain holidays a necessary release, perhaps, from the rigid formalities of middle-class family life in Victorian England. They enjoyed the chance to relax completely, to be as free-and-easy and as boisterous as they wished. They took their climbing seriously but, apart from a brief appearance on the scene of Aleister Crowley, who later became famous and widely hated as a protagonist of black magic and drug addiction, they seem to have been pleasantly free from the spirit of competitive acrimony. They were gentlemen and amateurs. They climbed for fun.

4 The Partnership in Action

This was the situation at the moment when Owen Glynne Jones and the Abraham brothers joined forces, and for the next three years their partnership dominated rock climbing. The special climbing qualities of the three men complemented each other as neatly as the Abraham photographs complemented Jones' prose in his book. Jones was already the leading figure at Wasdale Head. His strength and stamina were phenomenal, he was daring and dedicated, and his skill had developed with experience. He was the driving force. But George Abraham was quickly to become a fine lead climber in his own right, not so muscular in the arms as Jones but a pioneering exponent of the new art of balance climbing which was to increase in importance as climbers ventured onto more difficult ground. He was bandy-legged—'couldn't stop a pig in a blind alley' was the family phrase for him—but able, nonetheless, to move with smooth, unhurried confidence on steep rock faces. And Ashley was the ideal anchor-man, patient, sturdy and reliable, cheerfully willing to offer head or shoulders if all else failed, and capable of hauling his fifteen stone—most of it concentrated around his middle—up anything the others could lead. The brothers were great enthusiasts, increasingly crafty in devising safety techniques, and both were willing to cede the route-making role to the man they called 'our indomitable leader'.

It is a tribute to the quality of their climbing that they earned a high reputation although they spent, in fact, very little time climbing together. In the summer of 1896 they all visited the Alps—for the brothers it was the beginning of a habit that was to last more than fifty years—but they were not together there. They were reunited at Wasdale Head at Christmas, when they had at least one Jonesian expedition, to Pillar's Shamrock Gully. The weather was atrocious, the rocks coated with ice, but Jones led them doggedly up the climb, sustaining one considerable fall but picking himself up to carry on as the sleet and the darkness closed in. It was midnight before they fought their way back to the Wastwater Hotel at the end of what George later acclaimed 'the most memorably exciting day I have ever known'.

They were together again at Easter 1897, in Wales. They stayed first at Dolgelly and Jones had the pleasure of introducing the brothers to the cliffs where he had started his climbing nine years before, the Cyfrwy Arête on Cader Idris (Plates 75 and 76) and the Great Gully on Craig Cau. Then they moved north to the little hotel at Pen-y-Gwryd (Plate 60), at the eastern end of the Llanberis Pass, which was already the favourite resort of climbers. Climbing in Snowdonia, under the leadership of James Merriman Archer Thomson, the headmaster of Llandudno County School, was on the move but was not yet as advanced as in the Lake District. Two routes were regarded as the outstanding challenges of the area. One was the forbidding chasm above the head of Llyn Idwal known as Twll Du, the Devil's Kitchen (Plates 71 and 72). The other, at the western end of the great cliffs of Lliwedd, was Slanting Gully which had defeated a number of strong parties and killed one man who had fallen three years earlier while attempting it alone.

Jones could not stay with them long. He had arranged to climb in the Lake District and, particularly, to attempt another infamous route, C Gully on the Screes above Wastwater. As he said goodbye to the brothers, he gave them, according to Ashley's account, a solemn warning: 'Whatever you do, leave the Slanting Gully alone.' The advice was as counter-productive as that given by J. W. Robinson to Jones the year before. On April 27th the brothers set off for Lliwedd telling everyone they were 'just going to potter about' and George led the way up Slanting Gully. That evening George described the climb in the famous 'Locked Book' which Harry Owen, the landlord, only allowed to be used for serious entries about 'mountain rambles, botany, geology and other subjects of interest connected with Pen-y-Gwryd'. The brothers met no serious difficulties until they reached the cave about four hundred and fifty feet up:

> After leaving the bed of the cave a short climb of ten feet gives access to a white granite ledge, partly covered with moss and grass. Above here is an awkward slab, where a shoulder helps the leader to keep well in the chimney for about 12 feet until some splintered rocks on the right afford a capital hitch for the rope. The second man joined the leader here and paid the rope out over the hitch, whilst the leader took an awkward step round an overhanging corner on to a good foothold. After this the climb continues straight up for 15 or 20 feet until the chimney narrows considerably, and is blocked by the rock on the right wall overhanging. The difficulties here were found to be severe. The right leg was jammed in a crack as long as possible, until a sloping handhold immediately below the grass and turf was reached—the body is then swung out on the small footholds on the slab on the left and the ascent completed on these and some good holds on the right wall of the gully to the top of the pitch. . . . Geo. D. Abraham (Keswick).

So when the Abrahams received a triumphant telegram from Jones announcing the conquest of C Gully, they were able to wire promptly back with their news.

It was an eventful holiday for all of them. On the day after the brothers' success in Slanting Gully, Jones finally completed his long seige of Kern Knotts Crack by climbing it without the assurance of a top rope, a rope, that is, held from above to save him if he fell. On the same day Ashley Abraham and Oscar Eckenstein, a powerful and ingenious climber and the only man strong enough of character to withstand the prolonged companionship of Aleister Crowley, led two women up Lliwedd by the Central Gully and West Buttress Route, duly recorded in the 'Locked Book' as 'a first ascent by ladies'. And during the same period, Eckenstein joined the brothers in a cautious reconnaissance of the top crux pitch of the Devil's Kitchen, an expedition that met with no success and was to lead to ill-feeling later.

That summer the Abrahams with a new friend, J. W. Puttrell of Sheffield, created the route on Scafell Crag which immortalises them with its name, The Keswick Brothers' Climb. Jones did not reappear at Wasdale Head until Christmas when, with his book newly published, he began to carry rock climbing into fresh fields. He took a tentative look at Botterill's Slab on Scafell, climbed the first forty feet and reckoned 'it will probably go some day when conditions are more favourable'. This was a pointer to the new direction the sport was to take, out of the gullies and chimneys and cracks and boldly on to the steep and airy slabs which demanded stronger nerves and extra refinements of balance and delicacy of movement. His definitive step came a few months later, in April 1898, when he picked a cunning way across the open face of Scafell Pinnacle by the line now known as Jones' Route Direct from Lord's Rake. At one point the holds for hands and feet became so tenuous that Jones was forced to take his boots off and throw them down to his companion, G. T. Walker, so that he could tackle, in his stockinged feet, 'fifty feet of perhaps the steepest and smoothest slabs to which I have ever entrusted myself'. The climb is now graded 'Severe'.

Three days later Jones led the Abraham brothers up Pisgah Buttress on Scafell. But soon after, attempting to repeat C Gully on the Screes, he took another of his tumbles. The Abrahams were climbing elsewhere that day and returned to the Hotel to discover him, according to George's account, in chastened mood:

'Promise me you'll never climb C Gully on the Screes! It's a deadly place!' Such were the words spoken one Easter evening at Wasdale Head by my late friend, O. G. Jones. We had come back from a strenuous day on the Pillar Rock, to find the famous enthusiast looking paler than the snows on the Pillar's peak. He was bruised and battered, and had his arms in bandages; it was at last evident that the mountains had asserted their supremacy.

The summer of 1898 found all three in the Alps again, but not together. Jones enjoyed a strenuous season with two guides, and the Abraham brothers made their first ascent of the Matterhorn. At Christmas, though, they were once more reunited at Wasdale Head and in a period of unrelentingly atrocious weather Jones contrived two epic adventures.

One took place in Iron Crag Chimney near Shoulthwaite Ghyll and is chiefly remarkable for the fact that Mr George Perry Abraham, in his sixties and with no previous climbing experience, rashly allowed himself to be persuaded to go with them. He must have regretted it bitterly. It was cold and raining and blowing a near-gale; water was pouring down the cliff; it was dark before the climb was half completed; and a large boulder, dislodged by George who was climbing second to Jones, narrowly missed his head. Even today and in good conditions it is not considered a pleasant route.

The second was more serious. Jones had set his heart on the conquest of Walker's Gully on Pillar Rock, a formidable problem, more than four hundred feet high, which had defeated many parties and is still graded 'Severe (Hard)'. At the Wastwater Hotel, Jones bided his time, waiting for the weather to ease a little. Finally, on January 7th, 1899, he set off up Mosedale with George Abraham and A. E. Field, a classics teacher from Bedford and a keen climber. Despite the cold and the wet and the icy rock—

perhaps, indeed, because of them—Jones enjoyed himself:

> If variety were charming, we had charmed lives. Up the next ladder we went, through one obstacle, over the next and 'chimneying' up between the third and the great wall, the leader using the shoulders and heads of his companions, their up-stretched hands steadying his precarious footholds, and their expert advice supporting him all through. And with it all the most sublime views outwards and upwards and downwards of Nature's simple and severe architecture, designed and executed in her grandest style.
>
> At last we came to the final obstacle, the limit of previous exploration. We had arrived at a little platform deep in the mountain, and three enormous boulders, one on top of the other, overhanging more and more near the top, had to be circumvented. There was no way behind them; the only possibility was to work up one side wall and climb past them. I flung off my boots and Norfolk jacket, expecting to give the second man a bad time standing on his shoulders at the take-off, and attempted to climb up a narrow fissure in the left wall. Unhappily it proved to be useless, and we were all supremely uncomfortable when it was discovered that I should have to descend again.
>
> Next the right wall was tried, and I blessed the previous three months' monotonous training with heavy dumb-bells. The strain on the arms was excessive. Fortunately, there was no running water there, or the cold would have been unendurable. At the worst corner, by hanging on with the right hand, and with the left looping part of my rope through the recess at the side of the boulder, a good grip was improvised. Of natural holds there were none on that smooth, icy wall and the loop was a perfect boon. Even a perfect boon is hard to utilize when hands and toes are benumbed and all one's muscles are racked with prolonged tension. But the loop served its purpose, and after a few more struggles in the crack a ledge was reached from which it was evidently an easy scramble to the head of the gully.

Jones' Lake District book had been a success and he was now planning a similar work about the climbing in North Wales. To further his researches, he assembled his friends there the following spring, including the Abraham brothers, Puttrell and F. W. Hill.

> We were a merry party at Ogwen that Easter of '99, George wrote later. Mr and Mrs Hill and some cousins of Mr Jones were staying at Capel Curig, and early each day, be the weather snowy, rainy or fine, their cycle bells were the first sounds to wake us in the morning.

They discovered the possibilities of the Milestone Buttress and climbed on Idwal Slabs and Tryfan and on the cliffs of Glyder Fawr, where Jones had a dramatic fall at the Chockstone Pitch in the Central Gully and was saved from disaster by a cleverly threaded rope. But their most creative work was in the Devil's Kitchen area of Clogwyn y Geifr. The Kitchen route itself had finally been done the year before by W. R. Reade and W. P. McCulloch. Now it was repeated with Jones leading up the cracks at the start of the Great Pitch and George moving past him to complete the climb by traversing to the right, Puttrell and Hill following behind. Shortly after this Jones led the Abraham brothers up a new route to the right of the Kitchen, Hanging Garden Gully. By the final day of the holiday there were only two of them left at Ogwen, Jones and George Abraham, and Jones had to be in Bangor by lunchtime. On their Hanging Garden Gully climb they had noticed 'a promising but terrific-looking crack that ran up the crags, parallel to our route and away to the left'. On this final day they got up early and by seven o'clock they were at the foot of the cleft. They had a hard struggle, Jones leading, and at one point George had to straddle the gully, with the waterfall coming directly down on him, while Jones used his left shoulder as a launching pad, but they finally emerged at the top of the Devil's Staircase with another new route to their credit. 'In the midst of our success,' George wrote, 'we little thought, as we took off the rope and revelled in the warm May sunshine, that our last climb together was over.'

They were, in fact, excitedly planning a trip to Kanchenjunga in the Himalayas at Christmas. But on August 28th Jones' leading guide slipped near the summit of the western arête on the Dent Blanche in the Alps and pulled two other guides and O. G. Jones down with him to their deaths.

5 Publication and Controversy

The death of Jones led to the full emergence of George as a lead climber. In May 1900 he led the first ascent of Crowberry Ridge on Buachaille Etive Mòr in Glencoe (Plates 81–85). In October he led a large party up the Great Doup Buttress on Pillar. And the following May he created the route that was to remain the brothers' favourite for the rest of their climbing lives, the New West on Pillar Rock (Plates 21 and 22).

One of the first friends they introduced to this climb was Geoffrey Winthrop Young who had just left Cambridge to begin his teaching career at Eton and who was to succeed them as the great publicist of the sport. Half a century later he described the occasion:

> George Abraham was a climber who interested me. . . . He was graceful to watch and, as I understood it later, he was one of the earliest of the home school to climb consistently by balance rather than grip. His acquiline profile and shock of wavy hair already silvering at the tips in youth, contrasted exotically with his sturdy Cumbrian legs. He led me up the Pillar by the New West climb, which he had just worked out with his brother Ashley, another climber of great force. Its intricate sequence of traverses and verticals, each one presenting itself as a happy surprise when all progress seemed stopped, and George Abraham's chuckling relish of my successive satisfactions, made this a most pleasurable day.

For the next few years, though, the brothers' attention was chiefly concentrated on North Wales. They acquired some of the notes O. G. Jones had been making in preparation for his book and they 'spent a good part of each succeeding year climbing and photographing in Wales, with the ultimate idea of putting into effect the wish of our late friend.'

They were helped by a remarkable discovery. From the summit of Scafell Pike on a day of superb winter clarity at the beginning of 1902 they looked south a hundred miles to the snow-topped Carnedds of North Wales and saw 'the extreme ruggedness of their northern fronts.' With the help of a binocular they descried the cliffs above Cwm Llafar, on the north face of Carnedd Llewelyn and the higher reaches of Craig yr Ysfa. They were soon exploring these long-hidden crags for themselves, particularly Craig yr Ysfa, and creating new routes including the Amphitheatre Buttress and the Nameless Rib. They also, in 1905, made the first ascent of the Monolith Crack on Cribin, following the line of the narrow crack all the way up, a remarkable feat for a man of Ashley's bulk. And on Glyder Fach, with their friend A. S. Thomson, they forced a fine route, Hawk's Nest Buttress.

In 1906 their book was published, *Rock Climbing in North Wales*. It was a family effort. Their father published it; their photographs illustrated it; and the brothers wrote half each, George dealing with the northern areas, the Carnedds, Tryfan and the Glyders, while Ashley covered Snowdon and the mountains to the south.

The book is similar to Jones' in size, format and manner. They followed his system of grading routes into four categories, 'Easy Courses', 'Moderate Courses', 'Difficult Courses' and 'Exceptionally Severe Courses'. And they tried, without complete success, to emulate Jones' prose style. Neither of them had his natural command of language or his ebullient flow of high spirits and both were inclined to resort to a rather forced facetiousness, exaggeration, or descriptive flights too 'purple' and poetical for modern taste. Even so, it is an entertaining and valuable book, packed with information about the Welsh climbing of those early days and conveying something of its spirit.

The spirit of their climbing was, however, radically different from that of their predecessors on the Welsh cliffs. For the Abrahams, rock climbing was a jovial and communal celebration; their approach was down-to-earth and physical; they enjoyed their triumphs and they enjoyed sharing them with others. The attitude was anathema to some of the established Snowdonia climbers, men like Archer Thomson and Oscar Eckenstein. For them climbing was a personal, private, almost mystical experience, more a matter of communion than of community, and something that might be damaged irreparably by wide and, from their point of view, vulgar publicity.

Eckenstein had, according to Aleister Crowley, 'an almost fanatical objection to publicity.' And Archer Thomson considered it enough, when he had made one of his many new routes, to insert a brief, dry account of it in the 'Locked Book' of the Pen-y-Gwryd Hotel. It is not surprising that men such as these should have resented the arrival on their territory of the Abrahams, who made no secret of their plans to bring out a book. And it merely made matters worse that the brothers, despite their regrettable attitude and the comparative rarity of their incursions, were able to bag so many good new routes. In the introduction to their book, the Abrahams describe, without rancour, the welcome they were given:

We have always found it most difficult to obtain accurate information regarding the newer climbs. The authorities, with a few notable exceptions, were very reticent, and gave us but little practical encouragement. Often we have started out for a gully on the strength of an assurance that it was a well-known climb, and almost as frequently have we encountered difficulties far beyond what were anticipated. In many cases these gullies had not even been visited. It is hoped that a perusal of the contents of this book will help future climbers to avert such contingencies.

When the book was published it brought an explosion from Eckenstein. At the annual general meeting of the Climbers' Club in 1907 he introduced a resolution the terms of which are not given in the Club's Journal but which led Ashley to stand up and express 'regret on the part of his brother and himself that what they had published had caused offence to Mr Eckenstein.'

References to Eckenstein in the book are, in fact, almost unanimously flattering, especially about his pioneering work on Lliwedd, and there is only one passage that could have offended him—that where George describes their expedition to the Devil's Kitchen in April 1897. The brothers had arranged to meet him there. Eckenstein was late so while they waited George prospected the final traverse, protected by a top-rope from Ashley, and established that it was possible. By the time Eckenstein arrived it was clear that if they could climb the cracks to the point reached by O. G. Jones two years before, the route was theirs. They suggested that Eckenstein might lead the first part, then George would lead through and repeat the traverse to complete the climb:

> Our leader then advanced to the attack with my brother close behind him, whilst I coiled the rope around a knob of rock and belayed them as they climbed up the slippery lower slabs. They soon gained the foot of the first crack which is about twenty-five feet in height, and with his right leg jammed in the crack Mr Eckenstein worked cautiously up it. I noticed that whenever he got beyond the reach of my brother's long arms he developed signs of discomfort and slid back to safety. This process was repeated several times. At last, when a piece of rock came suddenly away in our friend's hands at a dangerous moment, he made a precipitate retreat, and I clambered up to their level and tendered my sympathies.

George then had a try and, though he got a little higher than Eckenstein, he too was forced to retreat. It is made clear that the conditions were bad, the rocks wet and slippery. That is the extent of the story. It seems little enough provocation and the incident reveals more about the state of Eckenstein's sensitivity than anything else.

There were more serious matters at issue, concerning the ethics of publication and professionalism. There was a strong feeling in those early days that the sport should not be publicised, and it was shared by some of the Lake District pioneers. The Hopkinson brothers, for example, were reluctant to tell even fellow-climbers about their exploits and did not record them in the hotel book. And Godfrey Solly and his companions on the first ascent of Eagle's Nest Ridge gravely considered, on the way back to Wasdale Head, whether to let it be known that a route of such severity and danger now existed. The arguments against publicity were powerful. It would attract more and more people to the crags and make them over-crowded. It would lead to tragedy by inducing foolhardy young men to tackle climbs beyond their competence. And it would diminish one of the great attractions of the sport, the sense of personal exploration, of venturing into the unknown.

There was an emotional as well as a rational element in the case against the brothers. Publication, it was felt, smacked of 'brag'—the mark of the 'bounder'—and especially the type of writing which Jones and the Abrahams produced with their detailed and highly-charged stories of adventure. It also smacked of professionalism. Until now rock climbing had been the preserve of men in search of holiday relaxation. The Abrahams, however, were professional photographers; they took photographs of climbers in action and printed them for sale; now they were producing and selling books as well. It was the thin end of the professional wedge which was to work into all popular sports in the twentieth century, in most of them much more extensively and effectively than in rock climbing. In an age which regarded the 'gentleman amateur' as somehow inherently superior to the 'professional player' and which thought of sport as something which should not, in the final analysis, be taken too intensely—something in which the spirit was more important than the result—it was natural that the activities of the Abrahams should be viewed with suspicion and dislike.

The way climbing has developed in this century leaves little room to doubt that there was considerably more to these arguments than mere Victorian snobbery and exclusivity. But it leaves no doubt at all that the tide of history was running the Abrahams' way.

In one of his books, published a few years later, George said:

The modern popularity of British rock climbing owes its inception either directly or indirectly to the life-work of Owen Glynne Jones. His favourite theory was that all men should climb, and they would be the better for it. This was in contradistinction to the somewhat dog-in-the-manger idea which then prevailed, that the joys of the mountain were only for men of liberal education and of the higher walks of life. Would that he could see the fruition of his wish!

6 The Evangelical Years

The years up to the outbreak of the First World War were active and productive.

Both brothers were now fully engaged in their father's photography business. George occupied himself chiefly with the retail side of things, running the shop and making lantern slides, while Ashley, the better businessman, kept the books and travelled widely to secure wholesale orders. The continued development of tourism in the Lake District made it a going concern and the going improved markedly about the turn of the century when they introduced the scenic picture postcard to Britain. On a visit to Zermatt in 1898 they had seen picture postcards on sale, and promptly recognised the opportunity. Until then the smallest pictures the shop had sold had been one-shilling prints, eight inches by six, an inconvenient size for sending through the post. On their return to Keswick they reduced a dozen of their most popular Lakeland views to postcard size, put them on sale and were immediately successful. This trade flourished for the next sixty years with views like that of Derwentwater from Latrigg, Windermere from Orrest Head, the group of mountains above Wasdale Head taken from the western end of Wastwater, and—most popular of all—Ashness Bridge. They made postcards of some climbing pictures as well and George was amused to discover one of their views of climbers on Napes Needle on sale in the shops of Chamonix, masquerading as an Alpine pinnacle called the 'Aiguille de la Nuque'.

They found an exciting new sport, motoring. 'For seeing the glories of nature,' George wrote, 'the open touring car is supreme.' His Sunbeam Mabberley, with tiller steering, acquired in 1900, was probably the first resident motor car in the Lake District. Two years later its brakes failed at the top of a steep hill in Keswick and when it was halted by a wall at the bottom of the hill, George broke his collar-bone. His next car was an Alldays, a ten horse-power four-seater built by the Midlands firm of Alldays and Onions, and thereafter he had many motor cars, most consistently Humbers, and, in later life, Daimlers. In the early days he tackled motoring in the same spirit as climbing. 'The lower part of the old Honister Pass road,' he wrote, 'has several steep little pitches, and one awkward corner rather less than half-way up the ascent.' Many mountain roads were still unmetalled, gradients were steeper and corners more acute than they are today, and the family often had to get out and push. In June 1913, in a ten horse-power Humber, he made the first crossing of Hardknott and Wrynose Passes from west to east, the harder direction and a route that had defeated a number of more powerful vehicles.

Both brothers became family men. George married Winifred Davies, one of the Welsh cousins of O. G. Jones who had cycled up to Ogwen each morning from Capel Curig on that last climbing holiday of theirs at Eastertime 1899. She was a keen climber as well as being a woman of common sense and a happy temperament. A Bachelor of Science from London University, her more rigorous training, artistic and intellectual, made her an invaluable literary mentor to George. She turned his thoughts into acceptable English, checked and corrected his facts, and toned down his more outrageously alliterative or flamboyantly purple passages. They had two daughters. One of them, Enid Wilson, has contributed Keswick nature notes to *The Guardian* newspaper for twenty years or so.

Ashley's wife, Lucy Kennedy, was the daughter of the Congregational Minister at Cockermouth. Her great talent was for music and she and Ashley, a resounding tenor, helped to keep the family's musical tradition alive. They had four children, two sons and two daughters.

Ashley was the more convivial of the two brothers. He was a keen billiards player and a formidable opponent across the chess-board—he was twice Cumberland county champion in the thirties. He followed his father into public life to become a member, and later Chairman of Keswick Council. He was a regular and popular lecturer in the great cities of England, illustrating his talks about mountaineering with lantern slides. In the summer season he would lecture in Keswick, using slides to illustrate 'A Tour through the English Lakeland in Summer and Winter'. And in the interludes he and George and their father would enliven the proceedings with trios on the 'musical stones'—a rock xylophone they had built from volcanic stones, gathered from a small area between Skiddaw and Blencathra and carefully chipped until each stone produced a note of correct pitch. Their repertoire included 'Abide with Me' and 'The Harmonious Blacksmith'.

When the Fell and Rock Climbing Club of the English Lake District was formed in 1907, Ashley was asked to be its first President and at the first annual dinner, held at the Commercial Hotel in Kendal, in November, he made this declaration of faith:

> To me the steep chimney, the hard struggle up a vertical crack, the delicate balancing round an overhanging nose with a drop beneath one—as Kipling graphically puts it, 'as straight as a beggar can spit'—are still amongst the best things this world affords. At present it is the rocks that fascinate, and any slight justification I have for standing here in my capacity tonight lies in the facts that I am a rock climber and lover of our Lakeland fells first, and a mountaineer afterwards.

Ashley spent much time in the summer of that year, and the previous year, climbing and photographing in the Cuillin with two friends, Henry Harland and A. H. Binns, and in 1908 he published *Rock Climbing in Skye*, a natural successor to Jones' book about the Lake District and the brothers' joint book about North Wales and following the same pattern.

This was to be Ashley's only venture into solo authorship, but George, once launched on the career, proved prolific. In 1907 he published *The Complete Mountaineer*, possibly the best of all his books, an informative survey of the world mountaineering scene with a great deal of advice on technique and equipment. It is generously illustrated and dedicated to his wife, 'To Her Whom I met on the Rocks'. Two years later came *British Mountain Climbs*, a compact and factual guide to the rock climbing known at the time, and two years after that he produced a comparable treatment of the Alps, *Swiss Mountain Climbs*. Another work, *Mountain Adventures at Home and Abroad*, which appeared in 1910, was more personal and anecdotal in style, a collection of miscellaneous essays, descriptive and discursive. He also produced a couple of books about motoring, and three more mountaineering works after the First World War.

George's style has many faults. His writing is spattered with archaic, pseudo-poetic words like ''ere', 'perchance', ''twas' and 'verily'. His attempts at description are usually over-blown and cliché-ridden. He could not resist a bad pun: describing an autumn climb in Skye, for example, he writes, 'Our reception on the summit was a ''coolin' '' one', and speaking of Striding Edge on Helvellyn he refers to tourists 'of the honeymoon variety, who apparently find some difficulty in clinging to the edge and each other at the same time'. He could not resist a legend either and repeats as fact many apocryphal and highly unlikely stories. Even when recounting his own adventures, he exaggerates. He was more concerned to make his narrative colourful and exciting than to keep it strictly accurate. And he took no care to bring his information up to date. The most successful of his books, *British Mountain Climbs*, ran into five editions, the last one coming out in 1945. Yet despite all that had happened in British rock climbing in the intervening thirty-six years, the text remains unchanged, and readers after the conclusion of the Second World War were still being told, about Clogwyn du'r Arddu, 'It cannot be said that this imposing mass possesses much prolonged interest for the rock climber'.

When all these failings are admitted, however, it must also be admitted that George's books exerted a powerful influence, spreading interest in rock climbing and attracting new recruits to the sport. In 1920 two important books were published by other authors, Harold Raeburn's *Mountaineering Art* and Geoffrey Winthrop Young's *Mountaincraft*, but these were technical works designed for the further enlightenment of the already dedicated climber. Until the late twenties George's books, racy and readable and sometimes thrilling, were virtually the only ones to be aimed at the general reader. And many leading climbers of the twenties and thirties were influenced and helped by them. Colin Kirkus, a dominating figure in Snowdonia in the early thirties, went scrambling on the Arans in Wales as a young boy with a copy of *British Mountain Climbs* in his pocket. When Claude Elliott, who later became President of the Alpine Club, began his climbing career in the Lake District in 1909 with three Etonian friends, Hugh Rose Pope, Nigel Madan and Trevenen Huxley, they were armed with *The Complete Mountaineer*. And Herbert Carr, the begetter of many new routes in North Wales in the post-war years, had both books with him in the Flanders trenches in 1917 and was able to quote long passages from memory. And when he became a student his college rooms were decorated not with the usual Medici prints of the time but with prints of Abraham photographs.

If the books were powerfully influential, the Abraham photographs were even more so. They were unrivalled for their time, and can still stand comparison with the best black-and-white work of later climber photographers. Their objective was simple—to portray the true nature of rock climbing: the size and configuration of the crags; the climbing routes in sufficient detail to bring out the grain and texture of the rock; and the skill and daring and exhilaration of the climbers. The aim was straight-forward enough, but the task was far from easy.

7 Photographic Methods

Nowhere in their writing do the Abrahams give any account of their photographic methods. Perhaps they were safeguarding the mysteries of their trade; perhaps they simply thought it would not be of much interest to their readers. But there are men still alive who worked closely with them and remember their methods clearly, and fortunately the vital part of their equipment, the camera itself, survives.

The Underwood whole-plate camera which was their favourite throughout their fifty years and more of active photography—'our ubiquitous camera' as George called it—was taken over by George Fisher when he acquired the Lake Road premises for his mountaineering equipment shop in 1967 and is still occasionally used for publicity photographs.

It is nothing more, in fact, than a sturdy wooden box, about twelve inches by twelve and three-and-a-half inches deep when folded up, with a hole at the front for the lens and a concertina-bellows, made of fine soft leather, at the back. It was designed to record images on glass-plate negatives, which measured eight-and-a-half inches by six-and-a-half. A brass plate on the box says 'The Instanto Patent'. The camera was made by the Birmingham firm, E. and T. Underwood.

The method of operation was simple. The first problem was to find a ledge level and large enough to accommodate the photographer and the legs of the tripod, which were telescopic. The camera was then firmly screwed on to the top of the tripod.

The next thing was to select the lens. The Abrahams usually had a choice of three: a Taylor and Hobson 'Cooke' lens with a twelve-inch focal length and an aperture range from f6.8 to f45, which they mainly used for set-piece scenic shots; a German Goerz lens with the same range, which they took climbing; and a Ross wide-angle lens with a six-inch focal length and an aperture setting from f16 to f64. Whenever light conditions allowed, they stopped down to f32 to get all the detail as sharp as possible.

They did not use filters and this is why their photographs rarely show cloud formations. And they did not use an exposure meter, preferring to rely on experience to judge the required duration of exposure.

With the appropriate lens screwed into position, the picture had to be focused. At the rear end of the bellows there was a plate of ground glass and focusing was merely a matter of winding the bellows backwards and forwards, by rack and pinion, until the inverted image on the plate became sharp. The bellows were locked at that point, the ground-glass plate was lifted out of the way, the lens cap put on, and a glass-plate negative slotted in, ready for exposure. The Abrahams invariably used the Ortho-chromatic plate to achieve a less heavily-contrasted, more natural effect. It was, by modern standards, a very slow emulsion and required a lengthy exposure, but it produced negatives that were virtually grain-free and capable of being considerably enlarged without suffering any perceptible loss of quality.

The photographer now enveloped himself in the focusing cloth, a black shroud designed to prevent any unwanted light reaching the sensitive plate. When all was ready, focus and aperture correctly set, the subject of his picture frozen in some fine dynamic attitude, he would go round to the front of the camera and grasp the lens cap, whip it off quickly and count off in seconds the duration of exposure he wanted, then whip it back on again. On a dullish day the exposure might be as long as four seconds. If the picture seemed promising, the photographer would immediately slide a fresh negative into position and take the shot again with a slightly different duration of exposure. The decision as to which was the better photograph could be taken back in the work-room.

The aim of the Abrahams was to record the nature of rock climbing—to portray climbers in action, and to bring out the true quality of the rock.

The most important element in their expertise was patience. They were prepared to wait for hours until the light was exactly right. What they were after was a diffused brightness, not direct sunlight which would make the shadows too black and the contrast too strong. If it were too brilliant when all was ready, they waited for cloud, and it must have been one of the compensations of working on the mountains of western Britain that they did not often have to wait long.

The angle of the fall of light was also a matter for concern. If it fell from directly behind the camera, the effect would be too harsh and flat; if it fell too obliquely, the shadows would be too pronounced. The ideal was that it should fall across the photographer's shoulder at what was called three-quarter angle. And it was a rule with them, as with many professional photographers of the time, that the best results would be gained when the light fell across the operator's right shoulder, though there seems to be no good reason why this should be preferable to the left. The reasons, however, for seeking this marginally oblique fall of light are clear; it ensured clarity to the whole picture and just enough shadow to bring out the grain and texture and detail of the rock formation.

Their intimate knowledge of the mountains of Britain must have been a great help to them. They knew the character and alignment of the crags and the routes up them and could plan with some precision to be on the right climb at the right time of day, according to the season of the year. Even so, in matters of the weather, it is not man who disposes, and there must have been many days when they had to carry their rucksacks home again full of unexposed plates.

Their work involved danger as well as disappointment. In fact, in the whole of their long careers of varied climbing at a high standard neither brother ever sustained serious injury through falling. But they came nearest to it through photography.

The need for careful preparation, then possibly for a longish exposure, and then sometimes for a second exposure, meant that the subject or subjects of the picture might be called upon to stay perfectly still, looking composed but purposeful while balanced on the edge-nails of their boots on very small holds over a big drop. At such moments most climbers are anxious to move on quickly. George was cool and competent enough to meet the demands of photography without trouble but this was not true of all their subjects. In the North Wales book Ashley describes a photographic session on Dinas Môt Pinnacle when 'the dark rock necessitated a lengthy exposure, and when it was but half completed the "sitter" slipped off his holds'. The plate, Ashley remarks laconically, 'was hopelessly ruined'.

The danger was greatest to the photographer himself and, though it was not in those days normal practice for a climber to tie himself to the rock when stationary, Ashley quickly learned the necessity of doing this when taking photographs. The practice saved him more than once. In his book, *Rock Climbing in Skye,* he describes a photographic expedition to the great pitch in the Waterpipe Gully (Plate 94):

Binns and Harland traversed to the top of the pitch, and proceeded to dispose themselves in artistic attitudes for the photograph, while I chose a pinnacle of rock lower down which overhung the gully, and from which my camera had an uninterrupted view of the big pitch.

My position was somewhat exposed, so I took the precaution of attaching myself with a rope to the top of the pinnacle. It was exceedingly fortunate that I did so. I had just made an exposure and was putting the slide back into the rucksack, when a sudden gust of wind blew the camera over towards the gully. It was just slipping over the edge when I made a grab and caught it, but in doing so lost my balance.

A wild clutch intended for the top of the pinnacle, but which only succeeded in securing my focusing cloth, was followed by a hazy and hurried wonder what was to happen next, when all need for prayerfulness was removed as the rope tightened round my waist and held me suspended over the gully.

The focusing cloth itself could spell danger. The disorientating effect of spending some time under its dark canopy was well known. On at least one occasion, in the Dolomites, when Ashley had been taking his usual care over a picture of George, he emerged into the daylight and stepped backwards off the ledge. Once again he was saved by the rope.

8 The Later Years

The rest of the brothers' story can be quickly told. The business prospered, their families flourished, and they carried on climbing.

Both were spared the horrors of active service in the First World War, George because he had varicose veins, Ashley because he had previously suffered from tuberculosis. In 1917 the business was turned into a limited company with the brothers and their father as directors, and when he died six years later George and Ashley carried on as partners. In 1932 Ashley's second son, Geoffrey Perry Abraham, who was already pioneering high-quality colour photography, joined them on the board.

About the time of the First World War the brothers made a brief excursion into film-making. The episode might have been completely forgotten if Geoffrey Perry Abraham had not, in 1972, discovered a few rolls of thirty-five millimetre film in the attic of his Keswick home. When it was printed and edited together this turned out to be reasonably well-shot and surprisingly well-preserved film of two young men making two of the classic Lake District climbs, Napes Needle and Kern Knotts Crack; and also a short travelogue-type film—a Pathé Review with printed captions which showed a party of climbers, including George and Ashley, tramping across the fells, roping up, and then George leading an ascent of Napes Needle by the route known as the Arête. The travelogue film must have been made in the early '20s, but it is possible that the other shots were taken before the War—a note on the tin in which they were found gave the date as 1913.

In 1921 they became involved in the making of a feature film. A British company called Stoll Films went to Borrowdale to shoot a film based on A. E. W. Mason's melodramatic story of love and violence on the crags, *A Romance of Wastdale*. The star, Milton Rosmer, was terrified of heights and the other leading man, Frederick Raynham, was no climber either, so George and Ashley were conscripted to climb for the cameras on Falcon Crag just south of Keswick while the actors posed for close-up shots on harmless boulders at the bottom. Careful inter-cutting completed the illusion.

Although the brothers continued climbing for many years more, their days of making new routes were over. The last route of their devising was the North-east Climb on Pillar Rock (Plate 27), led by George in April, 1912. It is now graded 'Very Difficult (Hard)' and described as 'a classic route with good situations in the upper half'.

After the war a new generation took over, men like H. M. Kelley, C. D. Frankland and

Bentley Beetham in the Lake District and Colin Kirkus and Menlove Edwards in North Wales. They devised more reliable rope techniques and took to using rubber-soled boots for greater adhesion, and soon they were attempting and conquering routes which had seemed impossible to the pre-war pioneers.

The brothers adopted the new techniques but never reconciled themselves to the use of rubbers, which seemed to them somehow 'unfair to the crags', not 'real climbing'. Their last rock climb together was in 1936 when George led again the route he had created thirty-five years before and which they still loved best of all, the New West on Pillar Rock.

Soon after this George's wife died. He re-married in 1940 and the following year, at the age of sixty-nine, took his new wife to Glencoe and led her up another classic route of his creation, Crowberry Ridge.

In September 1946 there was a fire in the store-room at Lake Road where their precious glass-plate negatives were kept. Some of them were damaged by the heat, more were broken by the nozzles of the firemen's hoses or cracked by the force of the water. But the fire was quickly brought under control and, fortunately, many of the best negatives had been duplicated, so the loss, though serious, was not disastrous.

When Ashley died in 1951 his son, Geoffrey Perry Abraham, took over the full management of the financial and wholesale sides of the business.

In 1954 the Alpine Club, under the presidency of Sir Claude Elliott, made George an honorary member. It is the main honour the Club bestows and George was particularly delighted because he shared it with the conqueror of Everest, Sir Edmund Hillary.

Six years later George retired, and he died in the spring of 1965 at the age of ninety-three.

The business did not survive him long. In November 1967 Geoffrey Perry Abraham retired. After a hundred and one years, the oldest family photography business in Britain was closed down. The premises were sold to George Fisher for his mountaineering shop. The negatives of the Abrahams' landscape photographs were given to the Tullie House Museum in Carlisle. Their climbing negatives, several hundred of them, were given to the Fell and Rock Climbing Club of the English Lake District, in whose safe-keeping they remain to this day.

The People

Plate 1 'The Keswick Brothers', Ashley and George Abraham—a studio portrait taken in the late '30s, when their hard climbing days were over.

Plate 2 Owen Glynne Jones, their climbing leader and hero of forty years before.

Plate 3 Jones in action on one of his rare excursions on to Derbyshire gritstone.

Plate 4 Ashley leading a pitch on the Kleine Zinne in the Dolomites. This is the only picture of climbing outside Britain in this book and is included because it is also the only known picture of Ashley leading a climb. He was usually either behind the camera or . . .

Plate 5 . . . in a supporting role, moral and physical. Here he 'lends a shoulder' to his brother George to compensate for a shortage of footholds.

Plate 6 The location is the west side of Thirlmere in the Lake District; the date, the early years of this century before the road was metalled. Ashley sits in front, George at the back, and the driver is Andrew Sisson Thomson of Kendal, a fellow pioneer of rock climbing and of internal combustion. His motorised tricycle was notorious in its day and known as 'The Stormy Petrel'.

Plate 7 This is not an Abraham photograph. It was taken at Wasdale Head in 1893— before the Abrahams arrived on the scene —and is included because it shows some of the leading figures of the early days. The man on the left, between the two ladies, is Dr W. E. Sumpner who had accompanied Jones on his first visit to the Lakes two years before. Jones himself sits in mid-picture, a climbing rope around him. His sister Nellie reclines third from the right, and the couple at the extreme right are Mr and Mrs F. W. Hill. Mr Hill was a frequent climbing companion of Jones' and the sole survivor of the disaster on the Dent Blanche in 1899 when Jones was killed.

Plate 8 This, the earliest Abraham climbing photograph, was taken in 1890, probably by Ashley. George is leading their younger brother, Sidney, who was thirteen at the time, up the cliff adjoining Sharp Edge on Blencathra. They are successfully defying every rule of climbing safety: the rock they are on is loose and unreliable, they are climbing simultaneously so that if one falls the other must surely follow, and they are joined by a length of their mother's washing line. In later, wiser years, the brothers called this picture 'How Not to Climb'. There is, perhaps understandably, no record of Sidney doing any further climbing after this. He took to banking instead.

The Lake District

Plate 9 Wastwater is the District's deepest and bleakest lake. Around the valley-head the mountains are Yewbarrow on the left, the shoulder of Kirk Fell, then the Napes crags of Great Gable which dominate the centre of this picture, and, to the right, Lingmell and the slopes leading to Scafell.

Plate 10 Wasdale Head and Wastwater. This view was taken looking South-West from the upper reaches of Great Gable, the area of the cairn erected by the Westmorland brothers of Penrith in 1879 to indicate what they considered the finest view-point in the Lake District. William Wordsworth wrote of '. . . the deep valley of Wastdale, with its little chapel and half a dozen neat dwellings scattered upon a plain meadow and corn-ground, intersected with stone walls apparently innumerable, like a large piece of lawless patchwork.'

Plate 11 Kirk Fell and Great Gable, seen from Lingmell. The rock of this area is known to geologists as 'Borrowdale Volcanic'. Strong, reliable, generously-fissured and frequently inclined towards the vertical, it might have been specifically prepared by the slow and weighty forces of nature to meet the needs of the rock climber.

Plate 12 The Wastwater Hotel in the 1890s. Offering quick access to the cliffs of Pillar Rock, Great Gable and Scafell, the hotel, under its able and ever-tolerant landlord, Dan Tyson, became the natural meeting place for the pioneers.

Plate 13 The entrance hall of the Hotel, Easter 1895. For a few days each Easter, Whitsun and Christmas, the Hotel was entirely taken over by rock climbers.

Plate 14 The Barn Door Traverse in the Hotel's stable-yard is one early route which no latter-day climber can follow—the barn has been demolished. Here the prehensile Dr Joseph Collier of Manchester demonstrates the delicate crux-move to Mr A. E. Field.

Plate 15 Bouldering is the art of forcing routes of extreme difficulty on rocks so low that it does not really matter if you fall off. On the Y Boulder in Mosedale Dr Collier devised a refinement—climbing it the easy way but upside down. Once again, A. E. Field is the spectator.

Plate 16 Meanwhile, on Gash Rock in Langstrath, six routes are attempted simultaneously, one by a voluminously-knickerbockered lady.

Plate 17 Wintry conditions on Great End, looking towards Borrowdale and the Northern Fells.

Plate 18 Alpine mountaineering, the summer conquest of big snow and ice mountains, preceded rock climbing by several decades, but in the 1860s and '70s some of the more dedicated Alpinists went to the Lake District in winter to keep in trim for the coming season. The gullies of Great End were a popular resort.

Plate 19 Most ladies wore long skirts, despite the inconvenience, right up to the First World War, and everyone carried the traditional ice axe, three to four feet long.

Plate 20 The West Face of Pillar Rock. Standing above the Ennerdale Valley, on the northern shoulder of Pillar mountain, Pillar Rock is the only sizable summit in the Lake District which cannot be gained without some use of the hands. It was the focal point of early interest in rock climbing. First climbed in July 1826 by a local shepherd, John Atkinson, probably by the route which is known as the Old West, by the 1860s and '70s it had become a popular excursion for the adventurous—they left their cards in a bottle on the top and sometimes sang 'God Save the Queen'. In May 1901 the Abraham brothers and two friends created the New West climb, a classic and popular route some 290 feet long.

Plate 21 The beginning of the New West, which the current climbing guide book grades 'Difficult (Hard)'.

Plate 22 Nearing the top of the New West. The middle man is Ashley's third son, Harry. George Abraham led the first ascent and later described his party's feelings when they returned to their starting-point: 'We lay on the rocks tasting all the joys of glorious conquest. Gazing up at those gigantic crags, which had not yielded without many anxious and exciting moments, we felt we had gained a new friend whom to know was to love.' The brothers returned to the New West many times and in 1936 it was the scene of their last rock climb together.

Plate 23 The East Face of Pillar Rock.

1 2

3

6

7

9

11

12

13

14

15

16

17

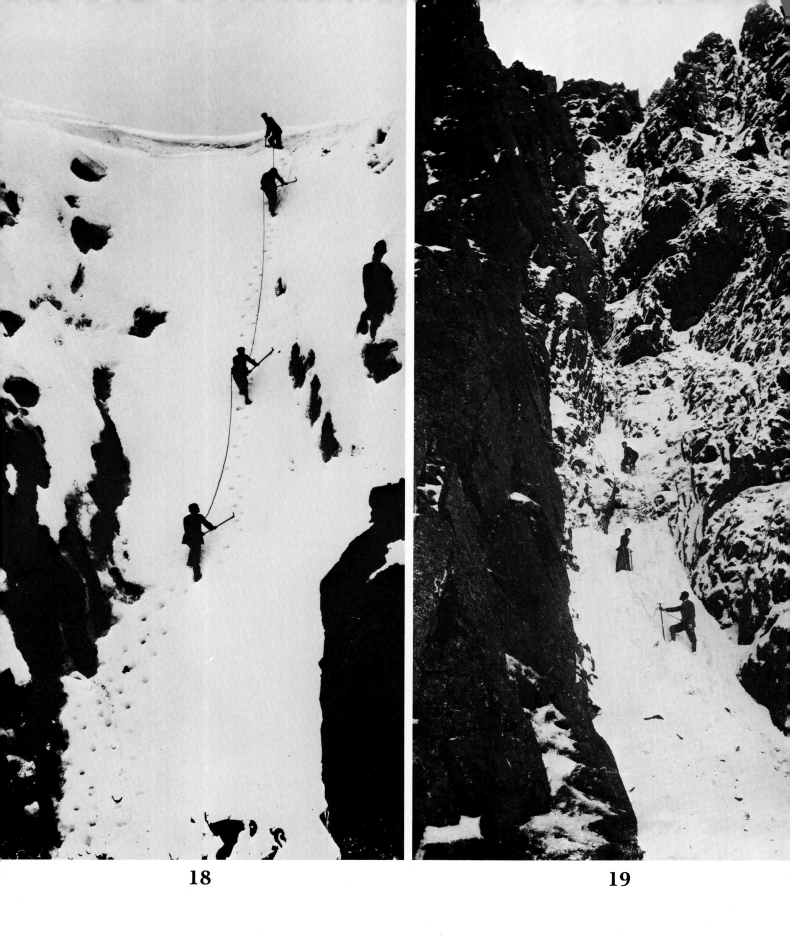

18

19

New West

Old West

20

Plate 24 Rounding the Notch on Pillar's East Face, part of the Slab and Notch route which has long been used as the easy way down this side.

Plate 25 The Stomach Traverse on the North Climb on Pillar Rock. The great pioneer, W. P. Haskett Smith, worked away at this route (320 feet of climbing in all) throughout the 1880s and finally completed it in July 1891. His route, however, by-passed the last and greatest difficulty, the bulging Nose.

Plate 26 The climber goes over the Nose on the North Climb, Pillar Rock. This, the natural direct conclusion to the route, was first done by Dr Joseph Collier, probably in 1893. His long limbs must have helped for the key is a high hold for the left hand and a long swing round the corner with the left foot. The pitch is short—15 feet—but still graded 'Severe (Mild)'. Haskett Smith had circumvented the problem by traversing left into Savage Gully, a manoeuvre he described as 'stooping to conquer'.

Plate 27 The North-East Climb on Pillar was the last new route discovered by the Abraham brothers in the Lake District. They did it, George leading, in April 1912. The climb is 420 feet long and currently graded 'Very Difficult (Hard)'. The darkly-shadowed recess beyond the climbers is Walker's Gully.

Plate 28 Two miles South-East of Wasdale Head stands the biggest cliff in England, Scafell Crag. Its long steep buttresses and deep gullies have been a favourite playground for rock climbers since the sport began.

Plate 29 The summit of Scafell Pinnacle, the last part of 'the easy way up'. The top man, cheerfully reeling his friends in, is John Wilson Robinson, the much-loved dalesman from Lorton and leading pioneer of rock climbing. He was the complete Lake District man, a formidable fell walker, an indefatigable climber, and the best of

company. He was persuaded to visit the Alps in 1898, was not impressed and never went again. He and George Seatree of Penrith introduced the rope to Lakeland climbing in 1885, but this picture shows how little security it afforded. By modern standards, everything is wrong. Robinson is not belayed, not tied to the rock behind him; he holds the rope casually in front of him instead of passing it round his back to increase the chances of holding a fall; and his two companions, W. Blunt and V. Blake, are moving simultaneously. Rope techniques remained dangerously rudimentary until well into the twentieth century and it is little short of miraculous that there were so few serious accidents.

Plate 30 A harder way to the top of Scafell Pinnacle. George Abraham, in a favourite hat and flourishing the nail-patterning of his boot, moves *à cheval* up the narrow ridge. The man above him is Gaspard, a professional guide from the Dauphiné who was hired by the Wastwater Hotel in the years before 1914 to 'conduct climbers on the various Climbs in the District at a moderate charge.'

Plate 31 Scafell Pinnacle and Deep Ghyll.

Plate 32 'We composed our limbs to a photographic quiescence,' wrote O. G. Jones, describing the taking of this picture (his full account is quoted in chapter one). The climb is Jones' Route from Deep Ghyll; the crag is Scafell Pinnacle; the date, April 20th 1896. It is the first Abraham photograph of a new route in the making. The route begins up the line of the curving crack, slightly to the right of the picture. Jones stands at the top of the curve, while George Abraham feigns a dynamic attitude below him. Ashley took the shot.

Plate 33 The crucial pitch on Moss Ghyll, Scafell. The climber, A. E. Field, is transferring his weight to the 'Collie Step', hacked in the rock by Professor Norman Collie on Boxing Day 1892. The problem had defeated several previous attempts. Now

Collie borrowed Geoffrey Hastings' ice axe and chipped a small foothold, then went on to complete the first ascent of the ghyll. In this picture the man behind Field is Dr Collier; the lower figure is A. D. Godley, a fine classical scholar, already a Fellow and Tutor of Magdalen College, Oxford, later to become the University's Public Orator.

Plate 34 Near the top of Moss Ghyll there is a choice of exit routes. This one is Collier's Direct Finish. The climbers are H. C. Bowen (above), C. W. Patchell, E. V. Mather, and an unknown friend of Patchell's.

Plate 35 Central Buttress on Scafell was first climbed in April 1914 by S. W. Herford and G. S. Sansom. The current guide book says it was 'probably the biggest single breakthrough in standard in the history of Lakeland climbing.' The route affords 475 feet of climbing of unrelenting difficulty; it is graded 'Very Severe (Hard)'; it is the most popular climb on Scafell. Soon after his first ascent Herford (who was to be killed in the trenches twenty months later) re-enacted the crux moves on the Great Flake for the camera, while protected by a top-rope from H. C. Bowen. Inset: the area where the action is, enlarged two times.

Plate 36 Napes Needle, at the foot of the south-facing crags of Great Gable, was first climbed by Walter Parry Haskett Smith in June 1886. He did it alone, by the route these climbers are following—the Wasdale Crack. It is a climb of 55 feet, today graded 'Very Difficult (Hard)'. To many people Haskett Smith's achievement marked the true beginning of rock climbing, and at Easter 1936 a crowd gathered to see him revisit the top of the Needle to celebrate the jubilee. He was 76 by then and did not, this time, climb solo. It is the photogenic quality of this piece of rock rather than the calibre of its climbing that makes it perhaps the best-known in England. Even so, the ingenuity of climbers is such that there are now eight distinct routes on the Needle.

Plate 37 The crags above the Needle, Napes Crags, afford a rich variety of routes.

Plate 38 The Arrowhead Ridge provides some of the crag's easier climbing.

Plate 39 The traverse on the Arrowhead Ridge, alive with activity.

370.

26

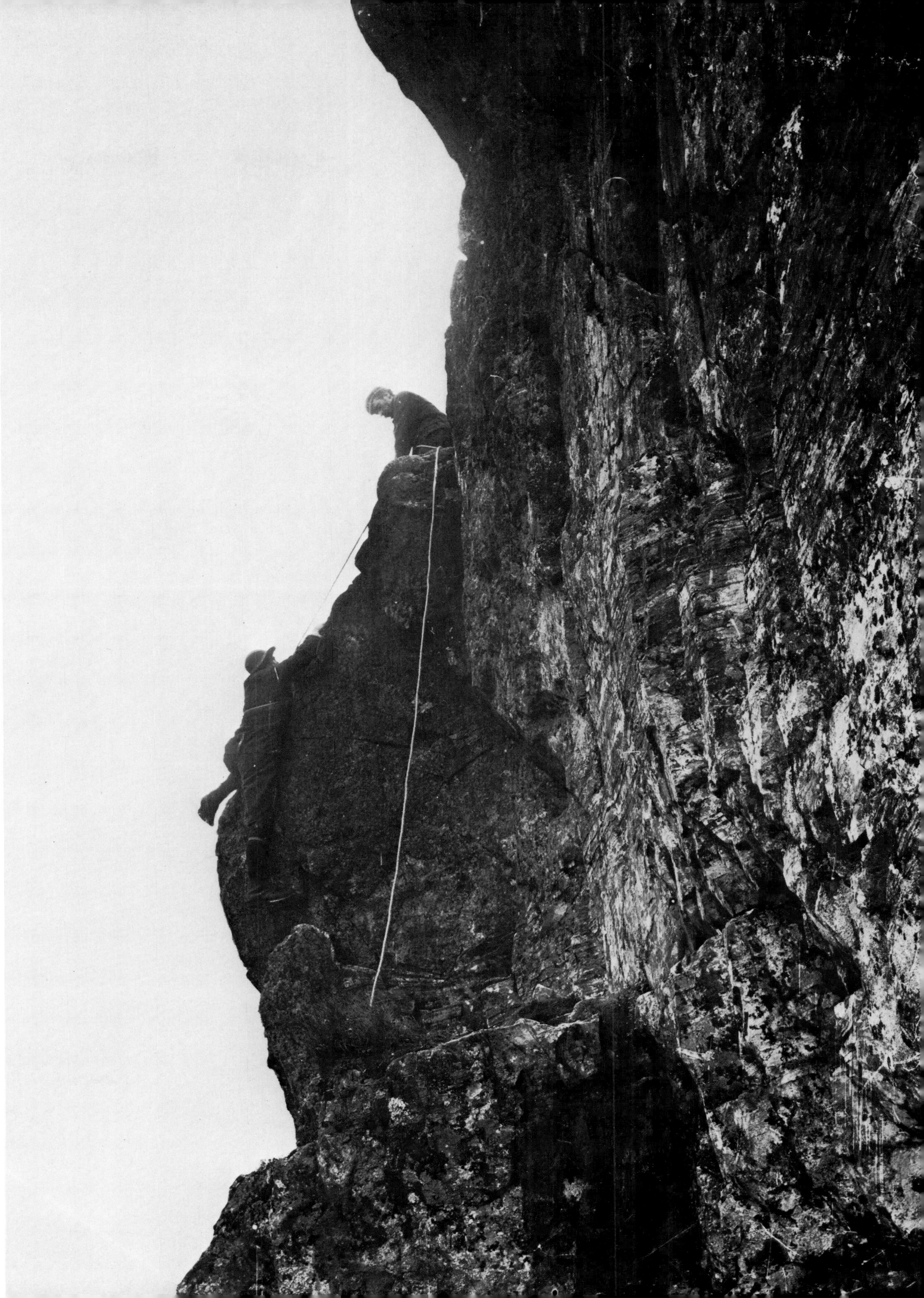

28

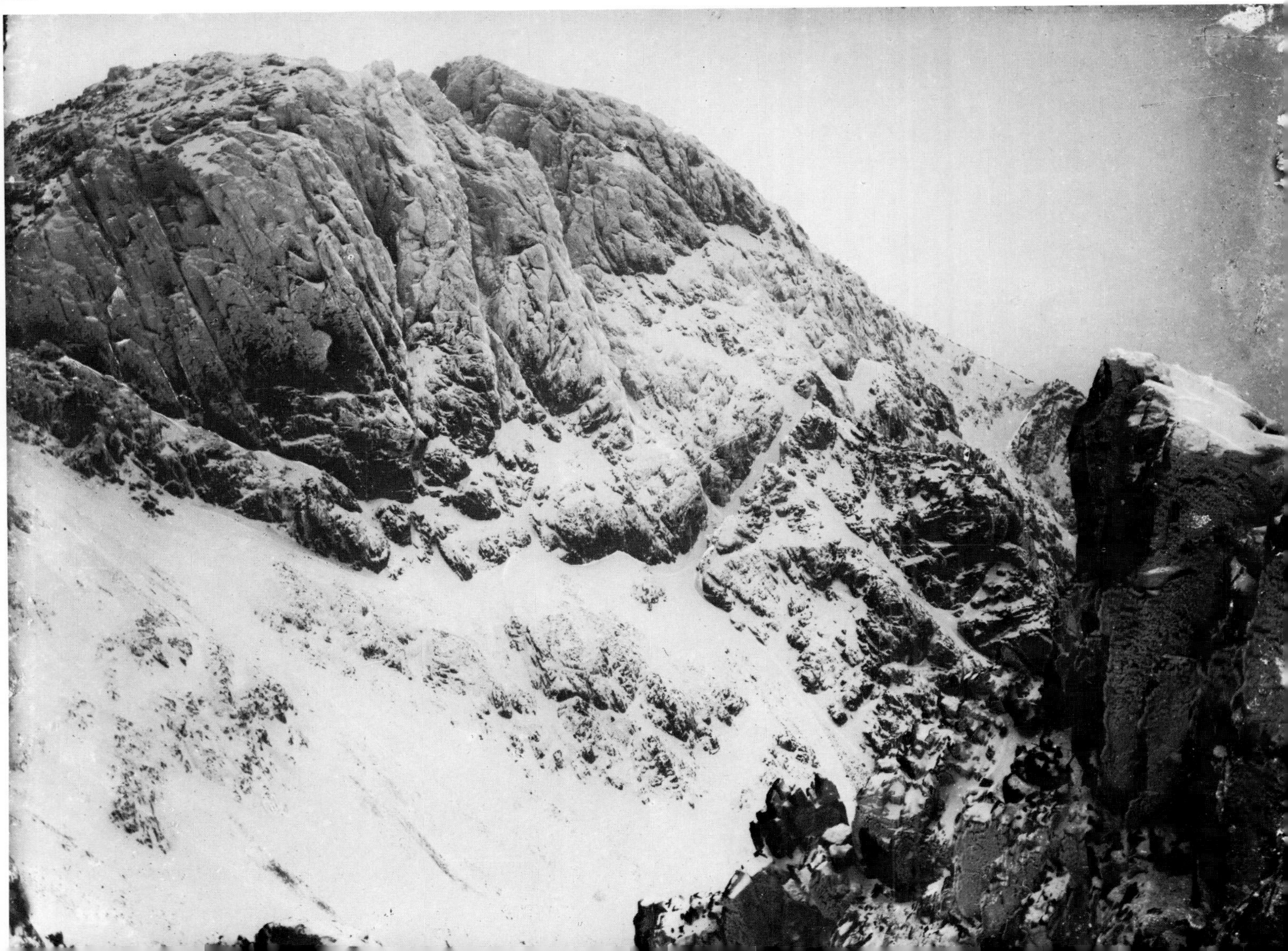

374.

Plates 40 & 41 Two action studies on Gable's Abbey Buttress. On the left George Abraham displays his bandy-legged style. On the right the second man struggles while the leader, unbelayed, passes the rope hopefully around a flake.

Plate 42 Eagle's Nest Ridge on Great Gable, the first route made on the crags which is still graded 'Very Severe (Mild)'. The first ascent by a party led by Godfrey Solly in April 1892 was a landmark. They were so awed by what they had done that afterwards, according to Solly's account, 'We felt unwilling to let it become known as a route to be followed upon our responsibility. We therefore left our advice on record that no-one should climb it unless he had previously reconnoitred it with a rope from above.'

Plate 43 Eagle's Nest Ridge is a climb of 120 feet. The current guide book describes it as 'a bold lead on good holds, with little protection'.

Plate 44 Kern Knotts Crack on Great Gable, only 70 feet but almost vertical and still graded 'Very Severe (Mild)'. Its conquest took O. G. Jones a considerable time. At Christmas 1895 F. W. Hill protected him with a rope from above while he inspected the top half of the climb. Next Easter he tried the ascent but failed three times at 'The Sentry Box', the wide section just below the climber on this picture, and only succeeded when he again had the assurance of a top-rope. But at Easter 1897 he led the whole route without a top-rope, H. C. Bowen following. According to legend, propagated by George Abraham, Jones then became so proficient that he could climb the Crack and descend Kern Knotts Chimney, just over the other side, in seven minutes.

Plate 45 George Abraham brings his second up to 'The Sentry Box' on Kern Knotts Crack.

Plate 46 It was left to a later generation to tackle the harder line of the Innominate Crack, just right of Kern Knotts Crack. It was first climbed in April 1921. The lead climber here is Stanley Watson, one of the first Lake District climbing guides.

Plate 47 Stanley Watson displaying his 'lay-back' technique on the route in the corner to the right of the Innominate Crack. This route, Sepulchre, was first climbed in June 1930. By this time rubber soles were in general use on dry rock. New equipment and improved safety techniques were making possible routes which the pioneers had never seriously contemplated.

Plate 48 On the northern side of Great Gable, Gable Crag overlooks the Ennerdale valley. Here George Abraham nears the top of the Central Gully route.

Plate 49 Doctor's Chimney on Gable Crag, first climbed by C. W. Patchell in 1896. It is almost a puzzle picture: find the four climbers. The dark tweeds the early climbers wore blended with the rock background. Despite this, even when the climbers were within the shadowed recesses of chimney or gully, the Abraham camera managed to record their outlines.

Plate 50 Dow Crag, seen across Goats Water. Climbers on their way to holiday at the Wastwater Hotel would sometimes take the train to Coniston for a day on Dow Crag before walking over to Wasdale Head.

Plate 51 Easter Gully on Dow Crag: the Cave Pitch.

Snowdonia

Plate 52 The Crib Goch ridge in the foreground leads to the summit of Crib-y-Ddysgl, then left to the top of Snowdon, 3,560 feet above sea level.

Plate 53 The Crib Goch pinnacles were a popular playground for the Snowdonia pioneers.

Plate 54 The Parson's Nose flanks
Crib-y-Ddysgl on the northern side. It was
named after 'the climbing parson', an
eccentric early fell walker whose passion
was to follow the skyline regardless of
obstacles and who may have made the first
ascent sometime around 1850.

Plate 55 The summit of Snowdon. The rack
and pinion railway from Llanberis to the top
was built in 1895, and the railway company
provided shelter and refreshment at the
summit.

Plate 56 The start of the East Buttress of
Lliwedd, the 800-foot cliff on the
south-eastern arm of the Snowdon
Horseshoe. Little visited now, it was the
favourite resort of Snowdonia's pioneer
'tigers'.

40   41

45

52

53

Plate 57 The West Buttress of Lliwedd was first climbed by T. W. Wall and A. H. Stocker in January 1883. Their route is not known. They recorded their achievement in the Pen-y-Gwryd Hotel visitors' book, and added, 'No-one is recommended to attempt the ascent without at least 60 foot of rope. Height of rocks = about 850 feet: time taken = four hours and a half.'

Plate 58 Lliwedd's Central Gully. Wall and Stocker tried this route in 1882 but were forced back after 200 feet. Lliwedd's great pioneer was James Merriman Archer Thomson who devised many routes, and in 1909 he and A. W. Andrews produced the first rock climbers' guide book, *The Climbs on Lliwedd*.

Plate 59 The height of Lliwedd's cliffs, their variety and broken nature, give the climber a greater feeling of true mountaineering—exploration and route finding—than any other crag in Wales or England.

Plate 60 There is probably no building in the world that has had a longer and closer connection with the history of rock climbing and mountaineering than the small hotel at Pen-y-Gwryd at the eastern end of the Llanberis Pass. Offering quick access to the Snowdon range, the crags along the Llanberis Pass, and to the Glyders and Tryfan, it has been a meeting place for mountain men for more than a century. The alpinist, C. E. Mathews, was a regular visitor from the 1850s onwards and founded the Society of Welsh Rabbits there to explore Snowdonia in winter. The genial hospitality of landlord Harry Owen attracted a later generation of climbers to the Hotel in the 1880s, and in 1898 the Climbers' Club was formed after a meeting of 'forty frequenters of the Pen-y-Gwryd'. Much of the history of rock climbing is recorded in the Hotel books; the signatures of many of the sport's great men adorn the ceiling of the bar; and modern visitors can still ease their weary muscles in a monumental bath which was installed about

1890. The present landlord, Mr Chris Briggs, has made few changes, and the Hotel looks today much the same as it did when this picture was taken. The step-ladders, which were to help visitors climb into the wagonette, are no longer available, and the hotel entrance was switched to the door-way on the left when traffic on the Capel Curig road grew too intense in the 1930s.

Plate 61 The Abraham brothers took this picture at Easter 1897, when they were secretly planning their attempt on Slanting Gully on Lliwedd. It shows, from left to right: (back row) C. Fox, unknown, Rudolf Cyriax, unknown lady, Miss Buss, and C. Legros; (middle row, sitting) Dr Collier, Oscar Eckenstein, Mrs Bryant, unknown lady, the Rev Septimus Buss, and A. D. Godley; (front row, on ground) Miss S. Nichols, the first woman to lead Kern Knotts Crack, and another unknown.

Plate 62 The Rev Septimus Buss waits his turn to tackle a short problem.

Plate 63 The Cantilever Rock on Glyder Fach.

Plate 64 Playful posing on Adam and Eve, the famous twin rocks on the summit of Tryfan.

Plate 65 The East Face of Tryfan, one of the best-loved mountains in Britain.

Plate 66 On Tryfan's Central Buttress.

Plate 67 The North Buttress of Tryfan with the Ogwen Valley beyond.

Plate 68 Climbing on the Milestone Buttress, whose potential as a climbing ground was discovered by O. G. Jones. Its situation, immediately above the tenth milestone from Bangor on the Capel Curig road, makes this one of the crags where climbing comes closest to being a spectator sport.

Plate 69 It was at Ogwen Cottage that the Abraham brothers enjoyed their last climbing holiday with O. G. Jones. Four months later Jones was killed in the Alps.

Plate 70 Behind Ogwen Cottage and only half an hour's walk away lie the dark waters of Llyn Idwal, with Idwal Slabs to the left, above them the cliffs of Glyder Fawr, and to the right of the stream the crags of Clogwyn y Geifr and the Devil's Kitchen.

Plate 71 The first pitch of the Devil's Kitchen, the Waterfall Pitch, being tackled by what John Menlove Edwards called 'the most proper route'.

Plate 72 The view from high up in the Devil's Kitchen at the foot of the final Great Pitch, with Llyn Idwal below and Llyn Ogwen in the distance.

Plate 73 The Llanberis Pass, looking north-west from just above Pen-y-Pass. The three fine crags immediately above the road on the right were scarcely touched by the pioneers and it was not until the arrival of Menlove Edwards in the 1930s that their potential was realised.

8.w.

60

61

62

65

69

70

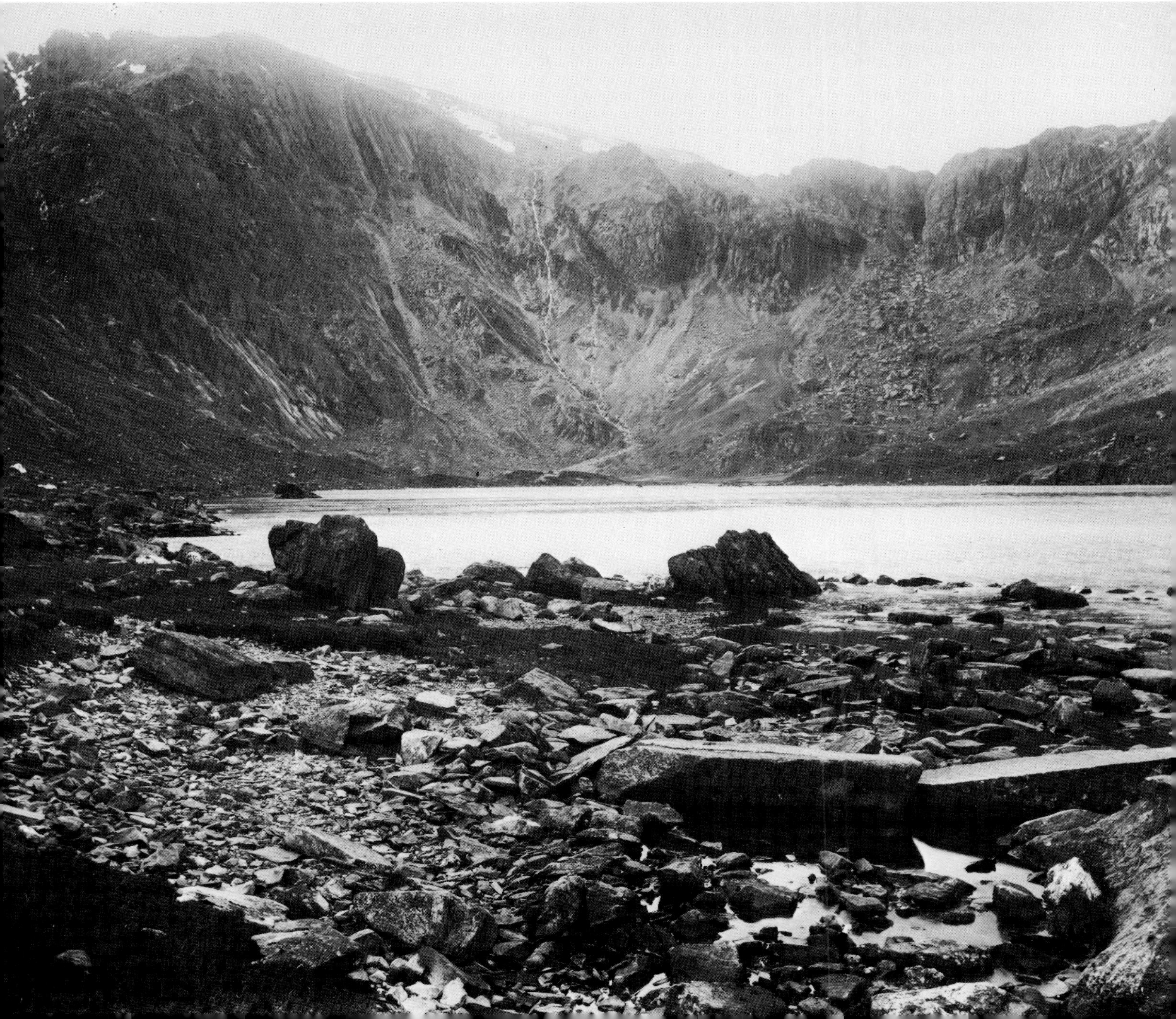

73

Plate 74 Clogwyn du'r Arddu, 'the black cliff of the black height'—affectionately known to modern climbers as 'Cloggy'—looms 600 feet above Llyn du'r Arddu the north-west flank of Snowdon. It has played a vital though intermittent role in the history of climbing. Perhaps the first British rock climb on record was made here in 1798 when two local clergymen, hunting for plant specimens, picked their way up the East Terrace, which slants up the cliff from right to left in the centre of the picture. More than a century later, in 1905, the Abrahams found a short route, the East Wall Climb, but considered 'Cloggy' basically uninteresting: 'The easy places are too easy,' they said, 'and the difficult places are impossible.' It was not until the late 1920s that exploration began in earnest, first with A. S. Pigott and Morley Wood of the Manchester Rucksack Club; then Jack Longland, Colin Kirkus and Menlove Edwards; and then, in the early 1950s, a fresh generation of Manchester 'hard men' led by Joe Brown, Ron Moseley and Don Whillans carried climbing into new realms of difficulty on this cliff and made it necessary to devise a further grade of route, 'Exceptionally Severe'.

Plate 75 The Cyfrwy Arête on Cader Idris was the scene of O. G. Jones' first rock climb. In May 1888, at the age of 21, he ascended the ridge alone, in un-nailed boots and without any previous experience. Nine years later, highly experienced but still enthusiastic, he introduced a group of friends including the Abraham brothers to the route. Ashley welcomed the flat top of 'The Table' as 'an ideal place from which to manipulate a camera.'

Plate 76 O. G. Jones brings two companions up the steep pitch above 'The Table' on the Cyfrwy Arête, Easter 1897.

Scotland

Plate 77 Glencoe. Writing about climbing in Scotland, George Abraham said: 'Of the mountain groups on the mainland those porphyritic sentinels, which stand in solemn grandeur guarding the wild and rugged Pass of Glencoe from the inroad of civilisation, demand foremost attention.'

Plate 78 The Sisters of Glencoe, mighty spurs of Bidean nam Bian on the southern side of the Pass. The Abrahams enjoyed both climbing and motoring in Glencoe.

Plate 79 The Collie Pinnacle on Bidean nam Bian, first climbed in 1894 when a powerful party—Professor Collie, Dr Collier, and Godfrey Solly—made a successful sortie into the Western Highlands.

Plate 80 Stob Coire an Lochan.

Plate 81 The great prow of Buachaille Etive Mòr which dominates the eastern end of Glencoe. It was here that the Abraham brothers, accompanied by Professor E. A. Baker and J. W. Puttrell, made their main contribution to the sport in the Highlands—the first ascent of the Crowberry Ridge, 600 feet of steep and exposed climbing. The narrow ridge, almost in the middle of the face, rises to a point just left of the summit.

Plate 82 The start of Crowberry Ridge. George Abraham, out of picture here, led the first ascent in May 1900. 'Until our visit,' he wrote, 'the direct climb had been left severely alone, and a certain authority had declared it to be impossible without steeple-jack's apparatus.' The four friends accomplished the climb, however, with no more help than their nailed boots and hemp rope. Ashley brought up the rear to take the photographs.

Plate 83 George Abraham brings the second man up the slabs on the Buachaille's Crowberry Ridge.

Plate 84 George contemplates the traverse. About this part of the climb, he wrote: 'The hand-holds were scanty and only just sufficient to make the balancing of the body possible. To add to the sensational uncertainty, the rocks were slightly moist at this point. After working carefully to the left for a few feet the foot-holds dwindled away to nothingness, and the only means of obviating defeat was to tackle the smooth bulge of rock that slanted upwards in an almost hopeless-looking manner. But the eye of faith descried sundry rugosities on the bulge, which eventually proved sufficient to help one defy the law of gravitation for a while.'

Plate 85 Nearing the top of the Crowberry Ridge. Ronald Clark and Edward Pyatt in their magisterial book *Mountaineering in Britain* describe the climb as 'a very daring tour de force of which few other parties then alive would have been capable.'

Plate 86 The north-western face of Aonach Dubh, overlooking Glencoe, with the legendary Ossian's Cave clearly shadowed, near the summit and to the left.

Plate 87 The North Face of Ben Nevis from across the Allt a' Mhuilinn. Tower Ridge, on the right, was first climbed in 1894 by Professor Collie's party.

Plate 88 The summit of Ben Nevis. The observatory on the summit was staffed from 1883 until the opening years of this century, and climbers could always look forward to shelter and refreshment from the weather-watchers.

Plate 89 On their way to Glencoe in 1900, carrying the news of the relief of Mafeking northwards, the Abraham brothers stopped briefly in Arrochar to photograph the Cobbler.

Plate 90 The Cobbler from the south. George found the climbing here disappointing although 'short, boulder-like problems can be unearthed, literally, on the prominent eminences known as the North and South Peaks.'

Plate 91 The Island of Skye. Behind the hamlet of Sligachan, Sgurr nan Gillean at the northern end of the great Cuillin Ridge.

74

77

78

79

80

81

Plate 92 In his book *Rock-Climbing in Skye* Ashley Abraham describes the Cuillin Ridge as '. . . continuous for miles and rising to fourteen peaks of more than 3,000 feet in height, the traverse of which presents all the various forms of difficulty that gladden the heart of a rock climber . . . The rock of which they are formed is ideal for the climber's purpose—rough, firm gabbro which affords magnificent holding for both hands and feet. As regards the rock-climbing itself it is, in my humble opinion, the finest in the British Isles.'

Plate 93 Another puzzle picture: there are three climbers on the South Face of the Bhasteir Tooth of Am Basteir in the Cuillin. Ashley wrote: 'The whole climb is strongly to be recommended. The actual difficulty, though never great, is always sufficient to engross the whole attention.'

Plate 94 The Great Pitch on the Waterpipe Gully of Sgurr an Fheadain. It was while attempting to take this photograph that Ashley slipped from his stance and was saved by the rope he had prudently tied to a flake, the incident described in chapter seven.

Plate 95 The Inaccessible Pinnacle which stands on the Cuillin Ridge on the shoulder of Sgurr Dearg. The name is impressive but misleading. There are at least six routes, of varying severity, to the top, and it was first conquered, by way of the easy East Ridge, in 1880. Two Lancashire businessmen-brothers, Lawrence and Charles Pilkington, who had been pioneering the art of climbing without guides in the Alps, visited Skye briefly that year and did the climb. Lawrence wrote: 'I shall always remember that as the noisiest climb I ever had. There was a foot or more of loose rock which had been shattered by the lightning and frost of ages. This formed the edge of the pinnacle and had to be thrown down as we climbed up. The noise was appalling.'

Plate 96 The upper rocks of Sgurr Alasdair, whose summit, 3,251 feet above sea-level, is the highest point in the Cuillin.

Plate 97 John Mackenzie on the slabs of Corrie Ghrundda, near the southern end of the Cuillin. Mackenzie was a native of Skye, started scrambling and climbing at an early age, and became the greatest of the Skye guides. His favourite and most frequent patron in a guiding career that spanned half a century was Professor Norman Collie.

Plate 98 The Cioch, high up on the crags of Sron na Ciche in the south-western corner of the Cuillin. Its existence was unsuspected until one late afternoon in 1899 when Professor Collie noticed its great shadow across the cliffs and deduced that it could be caused only by an unusual rock formation. The Professor, who climbed over many decades on big mountains all over the world including the Himalayas, loved the Cuillin best of all and returned to Sligachan to spend his final years. He died in 1942.

Plate 99 This picture of Chris Bonington on Kern Knotts Crack was taken in February 1974 with the Underwood camera. Arthur Dawson used the wide-angle lens, set the aperture at f32, and gave an exposure of $1\frac{1}{2}$ to 2 seconds. It was a dull day, heavily overcast. The plate was not the Orthochromatic which the Abrahams used but an Ilford Soft Gradation Panchromatic.

46.

An Excursion into Filming

(1) About the time of the First World War the Abraham brothers ventured briefly into film photography and made a short film of two climbers on Napes Needle and Kern Knotts Crack which Ashley used to illustrate his lectures. Then in the early 1920s they took part in a five-minute commercial travelogue which was shown on the cinema circuits as a 'Pathé Review'. This sequence of stills has been taken from the 'Pathé Review', which includes a shot of Ashley hand-cranking the Abraham movie camera.

(2) It begins with the scrambling up the screes above Wasdale Head.

If you're going to climb 'The Needle', you'll find one thing essential...

Pathé Review

(3) In best pre-talkie style, whole-frame captions indicate the story-line.

(4) The pattern of the boot nails expresses individual character . . .

(5) . . . and the climbers are introduced: George Abraham, his son-in-law Athol Weeks, Ashley Abraham with the rope and another man, unidentified.

'The Needle' is 2,600 feet high. Its base towers high above Waskdale Lake, in the valley below.

Pathé Review

(6) The caption-writing was shakier than . . .

(7) . . . the filming. Below the climbers, Wasdale Head and Wastwater.

(8) George sets off up the Needle by the Arête route . . .

(9) . . . and, without belaying, brings the next man across.

(10) George ascends the ridge . . .

(11) . . . on easy holds at first . . .

(12) . . . moving smoothly on those unmistakable legs.

(13) The hard part, . . .

(14) . . . getting on to this ledge, . . .

(15) . . . involves a final ungainly wriggle.

(16) Now the climb joins the original Wasdale Crack route, . . .

The top!

Pathe Review

(17) . . . so from here on . . .

(18) . . . it is familiar ground.

How the Camera Works

(1) The brothers started using the Underwood whole-plate camera in 1890. They worked it hard and almost continuously on the crags for nearly fifty years. And its period of active service is not yet over. On February the 17th, 1974, it was in action again on the old familiar ground at the foot of Kern Knotts. It made the journey from Seathwaite in its original rucksack (left foreground), a stout canvas bag with leather straps which comfortably accommodates the camera, two lenses, the focusing cloth and a dozen glass-plate negatives, with the folding legs of the tripod tied on the outside. Mr Arthur Dawson, who started work as an assistant in the Abraham shop in January 1929, demonstrated the operational procedure while Chris Bonington took this series of pictures.

(2) First, the tripod is set up. In the foreground lies the camera with the two lenses and their lens caps on top, and just to the right of it the pile of plates, already packed two to each wooden container. The containers are called 'book-form slides'.

(3) The camera is placed on the tripod . . .

(4) . . . and screwed into position from underneath.

(5) Then the body of the camera is lifted forwards . . .

(6) . . . and fixed upright.

(7) The lens, with its cap on, . . .

(8) . . . is screwed into the front, . . .

. . in this case, the Taylor Hobson wide-angle lens.

(10) To line up the shot and focus . . .

(11) . . . the lens cap is removed. The face of the camera, 'the rising and falling front', can be raised or lowered more than an inch . . .

. . . to enable the photo-
er to get the top or bottom
e subject in picture without
g to tilt the camera and so
distortion.

(13) To focus, the carriage is wound back . . .

(14) . . . until the image in the ground-glass focusing screen . . .

. . . is satisfactorily sharp.
eather bellows is the only part
e original camera which has
replaced—about 40 years ago.

. . . and the lens cap replaced.

(16) A final check on the focus is made under the cloth.

(19) Now the camera must be loaded. The ground-glass screen . . .

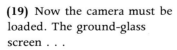

(17) Then the lens is set at the required aperture . . .

(20) . . . is unclipped and swung to one side.

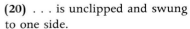

(21) The 'book-form slide', . . .

(22) containing two unexposed plates, . . .

(23) . . . is slotted in.

(24) With the cloth helping to keep out the light . . .

(25) . . . the sheath is lifted clear . . .

(26) . . . to expose the plate inside the camera.

(27) Everything is ready, plate, focus, aperture. The photographer smoothly removes the lens cap, . . .

(28) . . . counts off the duration of exposure he requires, . . .

(29) . . . and replaces the cap. Another negative is made.

Index

ABRAHAM, Ashley, 1, 17, 18, 20, 27, 29, 30, *Pl. 1, 6, 102*; as climber, 1, 4, 7, 11, 12, 16, 29, *Pl. 4, 5*; as photographer, 3–4, 7, 21, 26, 31, 37, 39, *Pl. 101*; background of, 6–7; as writer, 17, 21, 26; his family, 21; and Keswick U.D.C., 21; as lecturer, 21, *Pl. 101*; hobbies of, 21; as first President of the Fell and Rock Climbing Club, 21; death of, 28; *see also* Abraham Brothers

Abraham Brothers, 6, 7, 11–15, 16–9, 20, 29, 35, 38, *Pl. 1, 102*; as climbers, 1–2, 3–5, 7, 11–5, 16–7, 27, 28, 29, 30, 31, 37, *Pl. 5*; with Owen Glynne Jones, 1–2, 3–5, 7, 11–2, 13–5; as photographers, 1, 3–5, 7, 16, 17–8, 20, 24–6, 35, 38, 39; as writers, 16–9, 21; as pioneer motorists, 20, 29, 37, *Pl. 6*; later years of, 27–8; as filmmakers, 27, *Pl. 101*

Abraham, Geoffrey Perry, 27, 28

Abraham, George D., 1, 20, 27, 33, *Pl. 1, 102*; as writer, 1, 2, 12, 13, 14, 17, 18, 19, 21–2, 30, 37, 38; with Owen Glynne Jones, 1, 3–5, 11–2, 12–3; as climber, 1, 3–4, 7, 11, 12, 16, 18, 27, 29, 30, 31, 33, 37–8, *Pl. 5, 8, 30, 32, 40, 45, 48, 83–4, Pl. 102–3*; background of, 6–7; as pioneer motorist, 20–1, 29, *Pl. 6*; his family, 21, 28; later years of, 28; *see also* Abraham Brothers

Abraham, George Perry, 1, 6, 13, 17, 27

Abraham, Harry, 30, *Pl. 22*

Abraham, Ida, 6

Abraham, John, 6

Abraham, Sidney, 6, 29, *Pl. 8*

Allt a' Mhuilinn, 38, *Pl. 87*

Alpine Club, 9, 22, 28

Alps, 2, 5, 11, 13, 15, 22, 31, 35, 39

Am Basteir (Bhasteir Tooth), 39, *Pl. 93*

Amphitheatre Buttress, 16

Andrews, A. W., 35

Aonach Dubh, 38, *Pl. 86*

Arans, the, 22

Atkinson, John, 8, 30

BAKER, Professor E. A., 37

Barn Door Traverse, 30, *Pl. 14*

Beetham, Bentley, 28

Ben Nevis, 38, *Pl. 87, 88*

Bidean nam Bian, 37, *Pl. 78, 79*

Binns, A. H., 26

Blake, V., 31, *Pl. 29*

Blencathra, 21, 29, *Pl. 8*

Blunt, W., 31, *Pl. 29*

Bonington, Chris, 39, *Pl. 99, 104*

Boots *see under* Climbing equipment

Borrowdale, 1, 7, 27, 30, *Pl. 17*

Botterill's Slab *see under* Scafell

Bowen, H. C., 32, 33, *Pl. 34, 35*

Bowfell Buttress, 8

Bowring, F. H., 8

Briggs, Chris, 35

Broad Stand, 8

Brown, Joe, 37

Bryant, Mrs., 35, *Pl. 61*

Buachaille Etive Mòr, 16, 37–8, *Pl. 81–5*

Buss, Miss, 35, *Pl. 61*

Buss, Rev. Septimus, 35, *Pl. 61, 62*

CADER Idris, 11, 37, *Pl. 75–5*

Camera *see under* Photography

Cantilever Rock, 35, *Pl. 63*

Capel Curig, 14, 21, 35

Carnedds, 16, 17,

Carnedd Llewelyn, 16

Carr, Herbert, 22

Central Buttress *see under* Scafell

Cioch, The, 39, *Pl. 98*

Climbers' Club, 17, 35

    Journal, 17

Climbing
    Books, 2, 5, 14, 17–9, 21, 22, 35, 38, 39;
    Equipment: Boots, 9, 28, 31, 33, 37, *Pl. 13, 30, 46–7, 102*; Clothing, 9, 30, 33, *Pl. 19, 61, 62, 64*; Ice-axe, *Pl. 13, 18, 19*; for use of ice-axe *see* Techniques; Rope, 9, 37, *Pl. 13*; for use of rope *see* Techniques;
    Techniques, 9, 11, 12, 13, 30, 31, *Pl. 102–3*; *à cheval*, 31, *Pl. 30*; Alpine, 30, *Pl. 18–9*; bouldering, 30, *Pl. 15–6*; chimneying, 14, *Pl. 3, 49*; combined tactics, 4, 11, 14, 15, 29, *Pl. 5*; lay-back, 33, *Pl. 47*; simultaneous movement, 9, 29, 31, *Pl. 8, 18, 29, 39, 76*; stockinged feet, climbing in, 13, 14; stomach traverse, 31, *Pl. 25*; use of ice-axe, 30, 32, *Pl. 18–9, 55*; use of rope, 9, 14, 28, 29, 31, 33, *Pl. 8, 29, 41, 57, 102*; top-rope, 12, 18, 32, 33, *Pl. 35, 44*

Clogwyn du'r Arddu, 8, 22, 37, *Pl. 74*

Clogwyn y Geifr, 14, 15 (Hanging Garden Gully), 36, *Pl. 70*

Cobbler, The, 38, *Pl. 89, 90*

Coleridge, Samuel Taylor, 8

Collie, Professor Norman, 9, 31, 37, 38, 39

Collier, Dr. Joseph, 9, 30, 31, 32, 35, 37, *Pl. 14, 15, 33, 61*

Corrie Ghrundda, 39, *Pl. 97*

Craig Cau, 11

Craig yr Ysfa, 16

Crib Goch, 33, *Pl. 52, 53*

Cribin (Monolith Crack), 16–7

Crib-y-Ddysgl, 33, *Pl. 52*; The Parson's Nose, 34, *Pl. 54*

Crowberry Ridge, 16, 28, 37–8, *Pl. 81–5*

Crowley, Aleister, 10, 12, 17

Cuillin, 21, 26, 38–9, *Pl. 91–8*

Cwm Llafar, 16

Cyfrwy Arête, 11, 37, *Pl. 75–6*

Cyriax, Rudolf, 35, *Pl. 61*

DAWSON, Arthur, 39, *Pl. 104–6*

Deep Ghyll, *see under* Scafell

Dent Blanche, 15, 29

Devil's Kitchen, 12, 14–5, 18, 36, *Pl. 70–2*

Devil's Staircase, 15

Dinas Môt Pinnacle, 26

Dixon, Mary (Mrs George Perry Abraham), 6

Dolgelly, 11

Dollywaggon Gully, 7

Dolomites, 5, 26, 29, *Pl. 4*

Dow Crag, 33, *Pl. 50–1*

EAGLE's Nest Ridge, *see under* Great Gable

Eckenstein, Oscar, 12, 17–8, 35, *Pl. 61*

Edwards, John Menlove, 28, 36, 37

Elliott and Fry, 6

Elliott, Sir Claude, 22, 28

Ennerdale, 30, 33

FALCON Crag, 27

Fell and Rock Climbing Club of the English Lake District, 21, 28

Fenton, Roger, 6

Field, A. E., 13, 30, 31, *Pl. 14, 15, 33*

Fisher, George, 24, 28

Fox, C., 35, *Pl. 61*

Frankland, C. D., 27

GASH Rock, 30, *Pl. 16*

Gaspard, the guide, 31, *Pl. 30*

Gimmer Crag, 8

Glencoe, 16, 28, 37, 38, *Pl. 77–8, 86*; The Sisters of, 37, *Pl. 78*

Glyders, 17, 35; Glyder Fach, 17, 35, *Pl. 63*; Glyder Fawr, 14, 36, *Pl. 70*

Goats Water, 33, *Pl. 50*

Godley, A. D., 32, 35, *Pl. 33, 61*

Great End, 8, 30, *Pl. 17–8*

Great Gable, 5, 8, 29, 30, *Pl. 9–11*; Gable Crag: Central Gully, 33, *Pl. 48*; Doctor's Chimney, 33, *Pl. 49*; Kern Knotts, 1, *Pl. 104–6*; Kern Knotts Crack, 1–2, 12, 27, 33, 35, 39, *Pl. 44–6, 99, 101*; Kern Knotts Chimney, 33; Innominate Crack, 33, *Pl. 46*; Napes face of, 2, 29, 32, *Pl. 9, 11, 37*; Eagle's Nest Ridge, 2, 9, 18, 33, *Pl. 42–3*; Needle Ridge, 2; Arrowhead Ridge, 2, 32, *Pl. 38–9*; Abbey Buttress, 33, *Pl. 40–1*; Napes Needle, 3, 9, 20, 27, 32, *Pl. 36–7, 101–3*

Guardian, The, 21

HANGING Garden Gully, 15

Hardknott Pass, 20

Harland, Henry, 26

Haskett Smith, Walter Parry, 2, 5, 8, 9, 31, 32

Hastings, Geoffrey, 32

Hawk's Nest Buttress, 17

Helvellyn, 22

Herford, S. W., 32, *Pl. 35*

Hill, F. W., 14, 29, 33, *Pl. 7*

Hill, Mrs. F. W., 14, 29, *Pl. 7*

Hillary, Sir Edmund, 28
Himalayas, 15
Honister Pass, 20
Hopkinson Brothers, 9, 18
Huxley, Trevenen, 22

IDWAL Slabs, 14, 36, *Pl. 70*
Inaccessible Pinnacle, 39, *Pl. 95*
Ireland, 2
Iron Crag Chimney, 13

JONES, Nellie, 29, *Pl. 7*
Jones, Owen Glynne, 1, 2–5, 7, 11–2,
    13–5, 16, 17, 18, 19, 21, 29, 31, 33,
    35, 37, *Pl. 2, 3, 7, 32, 76*

KANCHENJUNGA, 15
Kelley, H. M., 27
Kennedy, Lucy (Mrs. Ashley Abraham),
    21
Kern Knotts, *see under* Great Gable
Keswick, 1, 6, 7, 20, 21, 27
Kirk Fell, 29, *Pl. 9, 11*
Kirkus, Colin, 22, 28, 37
Kleine Zinne, 29, *Pl. 4*

LAKE District, 1, 2, 4, 5, 7, 8, 12, 18,
    20, 21, 22, 27, 28, 29–33, *Pl. 6–51*
Langstrath, 30, *Pl. 16*
Legros, C., 35, *Pl. 61*
Lenses, *see under* Photography
Lingmell, 29, *Pl. 9, 11*
Llanberis, 34
Llanberis Pass, 11, 35, 36, *Pl. 73*
Lliwedd, 18, 35, *Pl. 59*; Slanting Gully,
    12, 35; Central Gully and West
    Buttress route, 12; East Buttress, 34,
    Pl. 56; West Buttress, 35, *Pl. 57*;
    Central Gully, 35, *Pl. 58*
Llyn du'r Arddu, 37, *Pl. 74*
Llyn Idwal, 12, 36, *Pl. 70, 72*
Llyn Ogwen, 36, *Pl. 72*
Longland, Jack, 37

MACKENZIE, John, 39, *Pl. 97*
McCulloch, W. P., 14
Madan, Nigel, 22
Mason, A. E. W., 27
Mather, E. V., 32, *Pl. 34*
Matterhorn, 13
Mathews, C. E., 35
Mickledore, 8
Milestone Buttress, 14, 35, *Pl. 68*
Monolith Crack, 16–7
Mosedale, 13, 30, *Pl. 15*
Moseley, Ron, 37
Moss Ghyll, *see under* Scafell
Motoring, 20–1, 29, 37, *Pl. 6, 77, 78*

NAPES Needle, *see under* Great Gable
Negatives, *see under* Photography
Nichols, Miss S., 35, *Pl. 61*
North Wales, 2, 4, 5, 8, 11–2, 14–5,
    16–7, 21, 22, 26, 28, 33–7, *Pl. 52–78*;
    see also Snowdonia
Northern Fells, 30, *Pl. 17*

OGWEN, 14, 15, 21
Ogwen Cottage, 35, 36, *Pl. 69*
Owen, Harry, 8, 12, 35

PATCHELL, C. W., 32, 33, *Pl. 34*
Pathé Review, 27, *Pl. 101–3*
Pavey Ark, 8
Pen-y-Gwryd Hotel, 8, 11, 12, 17, 35,
    Pl. 60–1
Pen-y-Pass, 36
Pettit, Alfred, 6
Photography, 3–5, 6, 7, 20; dangers of,
    26, 39; Abraham business, 1, 3, 6,
    20, 27, 28; Abraham photographs, 5,
    22, 23; quality of, 25; colour, 27;
    Ciné, 5, 27, *Pl. 101–3*; Lantern slides,
    20, 21; Picture postcards, 20;
    Tintypes, 6
  Equipment
    Camera (Underwood whole-plate),
      3, 24–5, 26, 33, 39; How the
      Camera Works, *Pl. 104–6*; movie,
      Pl. 101; Concertina-bellows, 24,
      Pl. 105; Emulsion, 25; Exposure
      meter, 24; Filters, 24; Focusing
      cloth, 25, 26, *Pl. 104–6*; Glass-
      plate negatives, 3, 24, 25, 28, 39,
      Pl. 104, 106; Ground-glass screen,
      Pl. 105, 106; Lenses, 3, 24, 39,
      Pl. 104–6; Lens cap, 25, *Pl. 104–6*;
      Tripod, 3, 24, *Pl. 104*;
    Methods, 24–6, 39, *Pl. 104–6*;
      Apertures, 24, *Pl. 105*; Exposures,
      24, 25, 26, *Pl. 106*; Focus, 24, 25,
      Pl. 105; Light, 25
Piggott, A. S., 37
Pilkington Brothers, 39
Pillar Mountain, 16, 30
Pillar Rock, 5, 8, 13, 30; East Face, 30,
    Pl. 23; New West Climb, 16, 28, 30,
    Pl. 21–2; North Climb, 31, *Pl. 25*;
    by the Nose, 31, *Pl. 26*; North-east
    Climb, 27, 31, *Pl. 27*; Old West
    Route, 8, 30; Savage Gully, 31;
    Shamrock Gully, 11; Slab and Notch
    Climb, 8, 31, *Pl. 24*; Walker's Gully,
    13–4, 31, *Pl. 27*; West Face, 30,
    Pl. 20
Pope, Hugh Rose, 22
Puttrell, J. W., 13, 14, 37

RAEBURN, Harold, 22
Raynham, Frederick, 27
Reade, W. R., 14
Robertson, James, 6
Robinson, John Wilson, 1, 2, 5, 9, 12,
    31, *Pl. 29*
Rope, *see under* Climbing
Rosmer, Milton, 27
Rucksack Club, 37

SANDBED Ghyll, 7
Sansom, G. S., 32
Scafell, 1, 5, 8, 29, 30; Botterill's Slab,
    13; Broad Stand, 8; Central Buttress,
    32, *Pl. 35*; Collie Step, 31–2, *Pl. 33*;
    Collier's Climb, 4, 9; Deep Ghyll, 3,
    7, 31, *Pl. 31*; Keswick Brothers'

Climb, 13; Mickledore, 8; Moss
    Ghyll, 9, 31, *Pl. 33*; Collier's Direct
    Finish, 32, *Pl. 34*; Pisgah Buttress,
    13; Scafell Crag, 31, *Pl. 28*; Scafell
    Pinnacle, 31, *Pl. 29–31*; by Jones'
    Route from Deep Ghyll, 3–4, 31,
    Pl. 32; by Jones' Route Direct from
    Lord's Rake, 13; Slingsby's Chimney,
    9
Scafell Pike, 16
Scotland, 5, 37–9, *Pl. 77–98*; *see also*
    Skye
Screes, Wastwater, 12, 13
Seatree, George, 9, 31
Sgurr Alasdair, 39, *Pl. 96*
Sgurr an Fheadain, 39, *Pl. 94*
Sgurr Dearg, 39, *Pl. 95*
Sgurr nan Gillean, 38, *Pl. 91*
Sharp Edge, 29, *Pl. 8*
Shoulthwaite Ghyll, 13
Skiddaw, 21
Skye, 22, 26, 38–9, *Pl. 91–8*
Sligachan, 38, 39, *Pl. 91*
Slingsby, Cecil, 9
Snowdon, 8, 17, 33, 34, 35, 37, *Pl. 52,
    55*
Snowdonia, 8, 12, 17, 22, 33–7,
    Pl. 52–74; *see also* North Wales
Solly, Godfrey, 9, 18, 33, 37
Sron na Ciche, 39, *Pl. 98*
Stob Coire an Lochan, 37, *Pl. 80*
Stocker, A. H., 35
Stoll Films, 27
Striding Edge, 22
Sty Head Pass, 1
Sumpner, Dr. W. E., 29, *Pl. 7*

THIRLMERE, 29, *Pl. 6*
Thomson, Andrew Sisson, 17, 29, *Pl. 6*
Thomson, James Merriman Archer, 12,
    17, 35
Tintypes, *see under* Photography
Tryfan, 14, 17, 35, *Pl. 64–7*
Twll Du, *see under* Devil's Kitchen
Tyson, Dan, 8, 30

WALKER, G. T., 13
Wall, T. W., 35
Walla Crag Gully, 7
Wasdale, 1, 27, 29, *Pl. 10*
Wasdale Head, 1, 5, 7, 8, 9, 11, 13, 18,
    20, 29, 31, 33, *Pl. 7, 10, 102*
Wastwater, 20, 29, *Pl. 9, 10, 102*
Wastwater Hotel, 8, 9, 11, 13, 30, 31,
    33, *Pl. 12–4*
Watson, Stanley, 33, *Pl. 46–7*
Weeks, Athol, *Pl. 102*
Welsh Rabbits, Society of, 35
Westmorland Brothers' Cairn, 29
Whillans, Don, 37
Wilson, Enid, 21
Winthrop Young, Geoffrey, 16, 22
Wood, Morley, 37
Wordsworth, William, 29
Wrynose Pass, 21

Yewbarrow, 29, *Pl. 9*
Y Boulder, 30, *Pl. 15*